W9-BMJ-316

THE LIBERAL CHRISTIANS

BX9843
W78
L5
1970

THE
LIBERAL CHRISTIANS
ESSAYS ON
AMERICAN UNITARIAN
HISTORY

BY
CONRAD WRIGHT

BEACON PRESS   BOSTON

MAR 26 '71

158998

Copyright © 1970 Conrad Wright
Library of Congress catalog card number: 76–84801
Standard Book Number: 8070–1670–5
Published simultaneously in Canada by Saunders of Toronto, Ltd.
Beacon Press books are published under the auspices
of the Unitarian Universalist Association
All rights reserved
Printed in the United States of America

For Elizabeth

CONTENTS

Foreword   vii

1   Rational Religion in Eighteeth-Century America   1

2   The Rediscovery of Channing   22

3   Emerson, Barzillai Frost, and the Divinity School Address   41

4   The Minister as Reformer   62

5   Henry W. Bellows and the Organization of the National
Conference   81

6   From Standing Order to Secularism   110

Notes   124

Index   141

FOREWORD

When the churches of the Standing Order in Massachusetts began to
divide into two bodies early in the last century, the liberals preferred
to call themselves "rational Christians" or "liberal Christians." The
term "Unitarian" was, at first, an epithet used by their orthodox ad-
versaries. Two generations later, when Henry W. Bellows sought to
bring the Unitarian body into some kind of organic coherence, the
name that he urged, unsuccessfully, was "The Liberal Christian Church
of America." Between 1815 and 1865, however, the emphasis had
subtly changed. When William Ellery Channing used the term in his
controversy with Samuel Worcester, he meant *liberal* Christianity as
opposed to evangelical or orthodox Christianity. But Bellows wanted to
emphasize liberal *Christianity,* in the face of a drift towards "Radicalism" or "Free Religion." Provided this ambiguity is understood to be
lurking in the title, a book of essays dealing with this particular span
of American Unitarian history may appropriately be called *The Liberal
Christians.*

Two of the essays in this book appear in print for the first time.
"Rational Religion in Eighteenth-Century America" was a Dudleian
Lecture at Harvard in 1961; because of the nature of that oldest of endowed lectureships in America, I have not tried to remove all traces of
the occasion on which it was delivered. "The Minister as Reformer" is
a much expanded version of a paper delivered at meetings of the
American Historical Association in December 1960.

The essays on Channing and Bellows are reprinted from the *Proceedings* of the Unitarian Historical Society. The Channing piece has
been slightly amplified with material to show the difficulty Channing's
contemporaries had in placing him theologically in the earliest years

of his ministry. "Emerson, Barzillai Frost, and the Divinity School Address" first appeared in the *Harvard Theological Review*. "From Standing Order to Secularism" is one of two related essays published recently on Church and State; it was prepared for a publication of the Unitarian Universalist Association edited by George H. Williams, entitled *Church, State, and Education: A New Look* (Boston, 1968). The same approach to Church-State relationships, but with more pointed application to the present situation, may be found in "Piety, Morality, and the Commonwealth," in the *Crane Review*, Winter, 1967. The present essay was chosen as the more appropriate one for this collection, even though it may seem more limited in its implications.

Permission to quote from manuscript materials has been granted by the Director of the Massachusetts Historical Society and the Custodian of the Harvard University Archives. Emerson manuscripts were used by courtesy of the late Mr. Edward W. Forbes and the Emerson Memorial Association. Certain of the essays were read by Professor George H. Williams and Mr. Charles R. Denton, and I have profited by their comments. For reading the entire manuscript with painstaking care, I am much in debt to Mr. Ralph Lazzaro.

RATIONAL RELIGION IN EIGHTEENTH-CENTURY AMERICA

I

The eighteenth century is commonly known as the Age of Reason. As our textbooks say, the rise of modern science in general and the scientific achievement of Sir Isaac Newton in particular gave to men enhanced confidence in the power of reason to establish the basic principles of natural philosophy, moral philosophy, political philosophy, and religion. The imaginative genius of Newton unlocked the secrets of the laws of motion, and heavenly bodies and earthly bodies alike were found to conform to simple mathematical laws. The British moralists discovered that all men have the capacity to make valid moral judgments, apart from any special revelation of God's will in Scripture. Locke and his followers explained how human beings would never have abandoned the state of nature and entered civil society had there not been rational arguments to persuade them to do so. And the deists discovered the adequacy of Natural Religion, the tenets of which are established by human reason, without the assistance of any revelation whatsoever, save only the universal revelation of God's power in the Creation. As Joseph Addison phrased it:

> *The spacious firmament on high*
> *And all the blue ethereal sky,*
> *And spangled heavens, a shining frame,*
> *Their great original proclaim.*

Now, the trouble with this familiar characterization of the eighteenth century, with its emphasis on the triumphs of the human reason and with its rational arguments for truths customarily taken for granted or accepted on faith, is that it leaves out so much. For if the eighteenth century appears from one point of view to be the Age of Reason, from another perspective it is the Age of Sentiment. Who is to say whether Pope's *Essay on Man,* with its regular heroic couplets, is more truly an expression of the eighteenth century than Sterne's undisciplined *Sentimental Journey*? Which is the more typically eighteenth-century version of the social compact, Locke's individualistic and rationalistic one, or Rousseau's mystique of the general will? Which is more representative of eighteenth-century religion, the freethinking of an Anthony Collins or a Tom Paine, or the evangelical revivalism of the Methodist movement in England or the Great Awakening in this country? Surely, any adequate treatment of the eighteenth century must take into account both aspects of it. We may perhaps choose to say that the rationalism of the century is the dominant motif, and so the popular image or stereotype has some justification. But we should not stop there. We should try to understand each half of the century in relationship to the other.

This is particularly important when we deal with eighteenth-century religion, especially in this country, for a very curious situation exists in American scholarly discussions of the subject. For a number of reasons, a kind of division of labor has been established, so that one group of scholars has explored the deistic or rationalistic tradition in American religion, while a different group has dealt with the various manifestations of evangelical religion. Thus the two halves of the century have been treated in isolation; or, at best, the historians of each tradition have merely used the other as a sort of foil against which their own story might most effectively be told.

Consider for a moment some of the books by American church historians in which some attempt is made to present a broader picture than strictly denominational history. Professor Sweet dismisses Deism with one page, and gives no hint of any other significant kind of rational theology.[1] George Stephenson pauses only long enough to mention that Thomas Jefferson was a deist, and that Timothy Dwight preached against infidelity at Yale.[2] Clifton Olmstead allots four pages to Deism and thirty-six to the Great Awakening and its aftermath.[3]

Now it is entirely possible that this is the right emphasis, and that the number of pages has been properly allocated. But if that is so, what are we to make of the historians of American philosophy who write as though Deism had been the basic type of eighteenth-century religion and almost everything else was a kind of anachronistic survival of Puritan days. In Muelder and Sears's source book, for example, the section on the American Enlightenment contains selections from Benjamin Franklin, Thomas Jefferson, Elihu Palmer, Ethan Allen, Thomas Paine, and John Witherspoon.[4] President Witherspoon certainly looks rather lonely among all the deists. Professor Werkmeister's *History of Philosophical Ideas in America* similarly places the deists in the center of the stage. He gives less than a paragraph to Jonathan Edwards, but takes five pages to summarize Allen, Paine, and Palmer. "When the initial wave of enthusiasm and emotional fervor had spent itself," he writes, "the Great Awakening came to an end and, emotionally exhausted, the people of the colonies turned to Deism and its sober appeal to reason." Between the decay of Puritanism at the beginning of the eighteenth century, and the rise of Transcendentalism in the fourth decade of the nineteenth, Deism is the only religious development Werkmeister considers to be of consequence.[5]

It is perhaps natural that Deism should attract the attention of historians of philosophy. Even when they turn historian, professional philosophers retain a systematizing habit of mind. Natural Religion, or Deism, interests them as the most direct working-out in religious terms of two key concepts of the Enlightenment: Nature and Reason. The physics of Newton and the psychology of Locke were revolutionizing the mind of the West; and Deism was the clearest and most systematic expression of that revolution as it affected religious thought. It is certainly satisfying—at any rate, for pedagogues—to be able to contrast Deism with Puritanism, the Enlightenment with Christian orthodoxy, Benjamin Franklin with Jonathan Edwards, the eighteenth century with the seventeenth.

But what are we to do when confronted with two very different, indeed incompatible, versions of the same story? The church historians tell us that Deism is of small consequence—that it may be dismissed with a reference to Ethan Allen, Tom Paine, and Benjamin Franklin. The philosophers suggest otherwise; for them, Deism is eighteenth-century religion in its most typical form. Shall we accept the view of the philosophers, who tell us that Deism is all that was significant? Or shall we follow the guide of the church historians, who tell us almost nothing about it?

The historian of philosophy may of course choose to justify the amount of attention he gives to Deism in terms of its philosophical significance, rather than in terms of the number of people who accepted that position. To be sure, he may argue, there were not very many thoroughgoing deists in America; but there were important men among them; and anyway, the philosophical significance of a body of thought does not depend on a counting of noses. But this does not wholly clear away the confusion. For the awful doubt gradually develops that the church historian and the historian of philosophy are not using the term *deist* in precisely the same way. That Tom Paine was a deist, they all agree. But what kind of definition of Deism will include Cotton Mather, Charles Chauncy, Samuel Johnson of King's College, and John Adams? Yet all these men, and more of the same sort, were referred to as deists by Woodbridge Riley in *American Philosophy, the Early Schools* (1907).[6] What of Ebenezer Gay, Jonathan Mayhew, James Freeman, and William Bentley, who were described as "respectable deists" by G. Adolf Koch, in *Republican Religion* (1933)?[7] In short, the historians of philosophy assume that everyone who believes in the principles of Natural Religion is a deist, while the church historians assume that everyone who believes in the Christian revelation is, in some sense, a Christian—not necessarily a very good Christian by evangelical standards, but at any rate a part of the history of the Christian Church.

The uncomfortable fact, however, is that there were a great many Christians in the eighteenth century who also stressed the importance of Natural Religion. Their significance has been very much obscured by the tendency of historians of philosophy to suppose that they were really deists who did not understand the logic of their own position, and who therefore clung irrationally to certain traditional Christian doctrines at the same time that they accepted the cosmology of Newton and the psychology of Locke. This is very much the attitude of Professor Koch, whose book on *Republican Religion* we cited a moment ago. Even more damning, he suggests that they simply did not want to jeopardize their social standing by acknowledging that Natural Religion was really the main thrust of their theological position, just as it was for the hated and despised deists whom the eighteenth century called infidels.

The net result of the way in which Deism has been treated by the two distinct groups of scholars we have mentioned is to leave the impression that there were really only two effective alternatives for the eighteenth-century mind. One might plausibly be a follower of Jonathan Edwards on the one hand, or of Tom Paine on the other; but there was no intellectually respectable middle way. Between evangelical orthodoxy on the right and Deism on the left there was nothing but compromise and illogic. I propose to maintain, on the contrary, that the choice was not simply between Natural Religion and Christian orthodoxy, but that there was a viable middle way, which was widely accepted in the American colonies, just as it was in the mother country. And since this middle way was the one favored by Chief Justice Paul Dudley, it is, I trust, not alien to the spirit of the lectureship he established to devote a Dudleian Lecture to an examination of it and its historical significance.

There were, in short, two kinds of rationalism in religion in the eighteenth century. One was Deism, which maintained that the unassisted intellectual powers of man can discover the essential doctrines of religion: the existence of God, the obligations resting on men of piety towards their Creator and of benevolence towards one another, and a future state of rewards and punishments. For the true deist, these tenets of Natural Religion were enough, without any doctrines of Revealed Religion. The other kind of rationalist agreed with the deist that there is such a thing as Natural Religion, but denied its adequacy, insisting that it must be supplemented with additional doctrines which come to us by a special divine revelation of God's will. We shall never understand the religion of the Age of Reason until we recognize that, from the point of view of that century, the difference between these two kinds of rationalism was simply tremendous. We have been led to suppose that because both groups believed in Natural Religion, they were, after all, pretty much alike. It is historically much more nearly correct to say that because one group accepted the Christian revelation, while the other did not, the gulf between them was considered to be unbridgeable.

There is, unfortunately, no short and easy designation or title for this second group of rationalists. In discussing the British, rather than colonial, exponents of this school, more than half a century ago, Professor A. C. McGiffert referred to the "supernatural rationalism of such men as Locke, Tillotson, and Clarke."[8] Professor McGiffert doubtless had no thought of inventing a title for the doctrine they held; yet, for lack of a better designation, the term "supernatural rationalism" was picked up from McGiffert by John H. Randall, Jr., in his book, *The Making of the Modern Mind* (1926), and has since been used sporadically and irregularly by other scholars as well.[9] It is an awkward, clumsy term, and one could wish that some other term had come into common use.[10] But a clumsy name is better than none at all, and we have had to wait two centuries for this one, so we might as well make do with what we have. There is a magic about names; and if there is an entity without a common name, we fail to recognize that it exists. I would even go so far as to argue that the fact that Deism has long had an accepted name, while the other kind of rationalism that we are beginning to call "Supernatural Rationalism" has not, helps to explain why the latter has been so readily overlooked as a separate, distinct, and vigorous tradition in this country.

II

Now that we have named this second kind of rationalism, and thereby assured it of existence, we must subject it to detailed examination. Actually, Professor McGiffert's classic little volume, entitled *Protestant Thought Before Kant,* does an admirable job of expounding the Supernatural Rationalism of John Locke, Archbishop Tillotson, and Samuel Clarke. All three men were commonly read by colonials, and their works are frequently listed in catalogues of libraries on this side of the water. There is no single American who might serve as a representative or type figure for this tradition as well as any one of these three might. Yet, for our purposes, it is important to examine the writings of American supernatural rationalists, even if it means consulting the fugitive sermons of figures of the second and third rank. Only in this way can we appreciate the extent to which this body of thought was accepted in the colonies. We must ultimately reach the conclusion that Deism was of far less consequence in America than our philosopher-historians have supposed; and that Supernatural Rationalism was far more sharply defined, prevalent, and significant than any of our scholars, whether philosophers or historical theologians or church historians, have ever intimated.

For purposes of exposition on this occasion, there is no more appropriate basis than the early Dudleian Lectures themselves, given on the foundation established at Harvard under the will of Paul Dudley, Chief Justice of the Province of Massachusetts Bay, who died in 1751.[11] He was a public-spirited citizen, if an aristocratic and vain one. There may still be seen, usually overlooked by the busy passerby, the granite milestones that Dudley ordered to be erected along the highway from the meetinghouse in Roxbury where he worshiped to the college in Cambridge of which he was a loyal son. Each stone to this day is inscribed with the date and the bold initials, *P.D.,* as well as the number of miles from the townhouse in Boston. But the Dudleian Lectures are Dudley's chief memorial. Four subjects were prescribed, to be dealt with in annual rotation forever. They were: Natural Religion; Revealed Religion; the Errors of Popery; and the Validity of Non-Episcopal Ordination. This choice of topics is revealing of the fact that Dudley had no thought of encouraging theological innovation. He wished only that the accepted principles of his own time and place and party should be competently expounded, so that the undergraduates of Harvard College would be reminded, in the course of their four years of residence, of some basic and familiar truths.

The first two topics—Natural Religion and Revealed Religion—are of course the ones with which we are particularly concerned. The first of these, in Dudley's own words, was "for the proving, explaining, and proper Use and Improvement of the Principles of Natural Religion, as it is commonly called and understood by Divines and learned Men." This discussion of Natural Religion would be followed the next year by "the Confirmation, Illustration and Improvement of the great Articles of the Christian Religion, properly so called, or the Revelation which Jesus Christ the Son of God, was pleased to make, First by himself, and afterwards by his holy Apostles, to his Church and the World for their Salvation."[12]

The President of the College was designated as the first Dudleian lecturer; and so, in 1755, President Holyoke undertook the proof of Natural Religion. Holyoke was a moderate Calvinist, a good representative of the tolerant and catholic spirit that prevailed at Harvard in mid-century.[13] In 1741, he had preached the annual Convention Sermon, in which he warned the clergy against "the *Deists* and *Free-Thinkers* of the present Age, who pretend to disbelieve all Revelation from God."[14] Now, in 1755, he set out to prove that there is such a thing as Natural Religion, which he defined as: "that regard to a Divine Being or God which Men arrive at, by mere Principles of natural Reason, as it is improveable, by tho't, consideration & Experience, without the help of Revelation." The essential principles of Natural Religion, Holyoke thought, might be discovered in the writings of virtuous heathen, like Cicero and Seneca. Turning to the writings of such men, who never knew the gospel of Christ, Holyoke found clearly expressed a belief in the existence of God and certain of his attributes, especially his goodness and his justice. He also found a belief in "a future World, a Future Judgment & Retribution, according to the Actions of Men."[15]

The belief of the heathen philosophers in the existence of God, as Holyoke saw it, was based chiefly on the argument from first cause. They were led to this belief "from the Excellency of the make & Formation of things, so wisely adapted to the Use of the Inhabitants of it. . . . there is such an Elegance & Beauty in all natural things, & such a regular order & subserviency, wherein they stand, to one another . . . from which it may well & indeed was inferr'd by the Heathen Themselves, That they were the Produce of some wise Agent. . . ." In short, "in the Frame of the Universe, there are numberless Evidences, that unanswerably demonstrate, the Being & Perfections of God, so as little, is it to be doubted that the rational Powers of the humane Nature, are capable of receiving those Evidences whereby the Mind cannot fail to be overpower'd with immediate inward Conviction, That God is to be worshiped, & an Homage paid to him as our Creator & Maker."[16]

The doctrine that Holyoke is here expounding is no different from the doctrine of Natural Religion advanced by freethinkers or deists in England at the same time. It derived its persuasiveness, obviously, from the current Newtonian world view, with its image of the frame of Nature marvellously fitted together so that the stars and planets revolve harmoniously in their courses; and also from the current epistemology of John Locke, which declared that our experience of the material world, as ordered by our rational faculties, is the primary source of all knowledge, including the knowledge of the Creator of the world that Newton had brought into view. The similarity between Holyoke's argument and that of the deists bothered him not a whit; for the difficulty the supernatural rationalists had with the deists was not the doctrines they affirmed, but those they failed to affirm; not Natural Religion, but the omission of a structure of Revealed Religion on top of it; not the rational proofs for the existence of God, but the failure to go on to a rational demonstration of the evidences of the Christian revelation.

Four years after Holyoke's lecture, the topic of Natural Religion was not assigned to another Calvinist, but to an Arminian, Ebenezer Gay of Hingham.[17] Gay's definition of Natural Religion was the same as Holyoke's, however: "RELIGION is divided into natural and revealed: —*Revealed* Religion, is that which God hath made known to Men by the immediate Inspiration of his Spirit, the Declarations of his Mouth, and Instructions of his Prophets: *Natural,* that which bare Reason discovers and dictates . . ." Since Holyoke had stressed chiefly the rational proofs for the existence of God, Gay felt free to turn to a rational demonstration of the principles of morality. "In the due Exercise of their natural Faculties," he declared, "Men are capable of attaining some Knowledge of God's Will, and their Duty, manifested in his Works, as if it were written in legible Characters on the Tables of their Hearts."[18] As an Arminian, Gay found this topic especially congenial; for he was able to intimate that the natural man had some ability to do God's will, as well as to discover what it is.

Four years later, in 1763, the topic was assigned to a Calvinist once more, the Reverend Peter Clark of Danvers.[19] His was a somewhat less optimistic version of the doctrine than the two previous; for while Clark agreed that it is "by means of the rational powers of man's soul, that he is capable of religion and morality, of the knowledge of the great author of his being, and of presenting a reasonable service to him,"[20] he was also impressed by the failure of men to use the rational powers they actually have. Natural Religion should be enough, but it obviously is not. Yet Clark argued that Natural Religion is an essential basis for Revealed Religion, since it is necessary to prove by rational argument that there is a God before we are ready to entertain the argument that Christianity was divinely ordained by him. In 1767, when the Reverend Samuel Cooke was the lecturer, this point was reiterated.[21] The proofs of divine revelation can be determined only by reason, Cooke argued: "as we must have an apprehension of the Being & Perfections of God, prior, to our receiving a Revelation as coming from him—it is evident that the Principles of Reason, or Natural Religion . . . are to be properly cultivated & improved . . . as the Foundation Principles, upon which Divine Revelation is Built, Established, & consistently admitted by us—"[22]

And so these lectures invariably begin with an assertion that men do not *need* revelation in order to discern the basic truths of religion; and they always end with an explanation of the fact that we nevertheless cannot do without it. One cannot claim "that Revelation is *absolutely necessary*," President Holyoke declared; "But this notwithstanding, Revelation is so *extremely necessary*, that without it, there is no Reason to think, That ever true Religion, if ever at first discover'd, should continue in the World, wch indeed is the Reason, That the World soon lost the Knowledge of God wch they had."[23] Even if we set aside all questions as to the effect of the fall of man on his perception of religious truths, it may be doubted whether the unassisted reason would reach the right conclusions about God and his attributes, without a long period of groping, and of trial and error. *We* know that God exists, because his revelation of himself reinforces the doctrines of Natural Religion; and the deists know that he exists, very likely in part because they have had the benefit of the very revelation they decry. But what of Adam and Eve on the day of their creation? Would they have immediately drawn the right conclusions from the existence of the sun, and moon, and stars? How long would it have taken them to work out the arguments from first cause and from design, if God had not revealed himself to them? As Ebenezer Gay remarked—rather naively, to our ears: "Had Man, with all his natural Endowments in their perfect Order and Strength, been placed in this World, and no Notice given him of it's Maker, might he not have stood wondring some Time at the amazing Fabrick, before he would have thence, by Deductions of Reason, argued an invisible Being, of eternal Power, Wisdom and Goodness, to be the Author of it and him; to whom he was therefore obliged to pay all Regards suitable to such glorious Excellencies? Would he so soon and easily have made those Discoveries, which are necessary to the Perfection of natural Religion . . . ?"[24]

Of course these were hypothetical questions; for the fact of the matter was that the Dudleian lecturers knew full well that the state of man is no longer innocent and incorrupt, but degenerate and defective because of Adam's fall. "Thus we see . . . the deficiency of the religion of nature and reason, as a guide to man's duty and happiness in his fallen state," Peter Clark declared. "This is not meant to throw the least disparagement on natural religion, the excellencies whereof have been in part reported; but to shew the necessity of revealed, that the former might more effectually reach its end."[25] Or, as David Barnes put it in 1780: "The depravity of human nature which early appeared, and that universal corruption of manners which took place soon after the apostacy, so obscured the light of nature, which in a state of innocency for ought we know, might have been sufficient; that mankind stood in need of some other guide in religion."[26]

In all this discussion, Natural Religion and Revealed Religion were conceived of as sustaining and supporting each other. "We should not depreciate and cry down Natural Religion, on Pretence of advancing the Honour of Revealed," Ebenezer Gay remarked, "as if they were two opposite Religions, and could no more stand together in the same Temple than Dagon and the Ark of God. . . . They subsist harmoniously together, and mutually strengthen and confirm each other. Revealed Religion is an *Additional* to Natural; built, not on the Ruins, but on the strong and everlasting Foundations of it."[27] Revealed Religion is as rational as Natural Religion, not in the sense that its principles are discovered by the bare use of the reason, but in the sense that reason accepts them and approves them as soon as they are known.

But it was not enough to prove that a special revelation of God's purposes would be of enormous advantage to weak and sinful men; it was also necessary to demonstrate that Christianity was indeed such a revelation. This was the concern of the lectures on Revealed Religion, which always came a year after the ones on Natural Religion. The first speaker in this sequence was the Reverend John Barnard of Marblehead, a close friend of President Holyoke, and, like him, a moderate and tolerant Calvinist.[28] The lecturers who followed him at the stated four-year intervals were chosen indifferently from the Arminian and from the moderate Calvinist groups, rather than from the more evangelical or Edwardean wing of the congregational churches.

The resulting body of apologetics rested firmly on Lockean assumptions. For one thing, the lecturers were aware of Locke's distinction between truths that are according to reason, those that are contrary to reason, and those that are above reason. These distinctions may be clarified by a simple example. An Englishman who had never traveled in the antipodes might be amazed to hear that in a far-off land there are animals which hop considerable distances on powerful hind legs, the females carrying their young in pouches. This is not in accordance with anything that life in England would lead one to expect; yet there is nothing inherently illogical or self-contradictory about it. Similarly, with religious doctrines: that we are saved through the mediation of Jesus Christ, and not in some other way, is not illogical or unreasonable, even though we might never have guessed that this is how God has chosen to save us, if it had not been specially revealed to us. That we should break bread and drink wine together in solemn recognition of the fact that the blood of Christ was shed for us is perfectly plausible; but it was necessary that this obligation should be made known to us by a special revelation. These doctrines are above reason, but not contrary to it.

The Lockean basis for this body of thought is seen in an even more fundamental way. The lecturers take it for granted that religious truths, like all other truths, come to us through sensation and reflection. They reject as "enthusiasm"—in the eighteenth-century meaning of that word—any notion of the communication of doctrinal truths by God directly, as in a moment of mystical illumination. That, after all, was the error of the revivalists, who mistook the products of overheated imaginations for revelations from God. When a religious enthusiast saw before him the image of Christ with blood streaming from his wounds, or heard voices speaking to his inner ear, he could only be suffering from a disturbance of the animal spirits.

When God speaks to men, as to Moses and the prophets, they hear him in just the same way that they hear the words of a fellow human being. Conceivably, God might speak again in New England as he once did on Mount Sinai; but the prophets of the Age of Reason had no wish to encourage people to think that this was at all likely. A direct revelation had obviously been necessary in Roman times to recover men from the depths of superstition that heathen polytheism had led them into; but New England needed no such extreme measures. Once the Christian revelation had been given to men, no further revelation need be expected, for none is required. But this inevitably means that our knowledge of the Christian revelation depends on the testimony of those who originally received it, rather than on firsthand experience. The hypothetical Englishman of whom we spoke will believe that kangaroos exist in Australia, even though he himself has

never seen them, only if he has confidence in the veracity and reliability of the person who tells him what he has actually seen at first
hand. Similarly, we accept the truths of Christian doctrine if we have
confidence in the veracity and reliability of Jesus Christ and the apostles,
through whom these truths were communicated to us.

Certain deists had argued that Christianity was "a cunningly devised
fable," constructed by priests who sought to gain control over innocent
but superstitious people. It was therefore thought necessary, if the
structure of Christian apologetics were to be soundly built, to start out
by proving that Jesus was actually an historical figure, and not a fiction
of priestcraft. Benjamin Stevens, who was Dudleian lecturer in 1772,
and David Barnes, who preached eight years later, devoted most of
their attention to this problem. "I shall attempt to prove," wrote
Barnes, "that there was such a person as Jesus Christ, that he was
born in the Augustan age; that after continuing some time in the
world, he died upon the cross. —That the history of Jesus Christ as
contained in the four gospels and the other books of the new testament, were wrote soon after the death of our Saviour, by persons who
enjoyed peculiar advantages for ascertaining the truth of what they
wrote —That they were neither enthusiasts nor impostors, they [were]
not deceived themselves, nor had they any temptation, that we can
conceive of, to deceive others— . . . That the gospel has been handed
down to us pure and uncorrupted without any material errors or mistakes."[29] It is hardly necessary to follow through Barnes's detailed
proof of these points. He argues that the gospels were quoted or mentioned by other ecclesiastical writers from a very early date; that the
writers claimed to be eyewitnesses of the events they record, a claim
that would have been overthrown at the time had it been false; and
that their manner of writing shows that they were acquainted with the
customs of the times. In all this discussion, Barnes does little more than
repeat material drawn from Nathaniel Lardner's multivolumed *Credibility of the Gospel History*.

The rational proof of Revealed Religion was now approaching its
most critical point—and its climax. It was not enough to demonstrate
that Jesus had actually lived, and was not a fiction of wicked and de-
signing priests. There had to be some conclusive evidence that he was
God's chosen messenger, entrusted with the task of communicating to
men the good news that there was a way of salvation despite the sin

and corruption of their depraved souls. When a messenger comes bearing information and instructions for us from some earthly potentate, we do not obey him without investigation; we ask for his credentials. We insist that he present evidence of a kind that can be seen or touched and rationally judged, so as to persuade us that he is truly the messenger he claims to be. Jesus Christ comes to us with such a claim, and we ask him for his credentials. This is how Thomas Barnard put it, in 1768: "When the Almighty *mediately* uses instruments, like ourselves, to convey his light and truth to us, they must be able to give convincing evidence, that they received their messages from God, and were ordered by him to publish them."[30]

The chief evidences of the truth of Christianity on which the Dudleian lecturers relied were that Christ fulfilled prophecies and that he worked miracles. Fulfillment of prophecy is of course not absolutely conclusive, but it is fairly persuasive. If an earthly sovereign announces that his messenger will appear in such and such a place at approximately such and such a time, and that he may be recognized because he bears a certain mark of identification, it is still possible for an impostor to appear in his place. But when someone does arrive who carries the proper identification, the presumption is strongly in his favor. And so John Barnard, the second Dudleian lecturer, in 1756, undertook to prove "that there was a certain Person, stiled the MESSIAH, who was spoken of, in the ancient Scriptures, as one to be sent from GOD"; and that "all those *Characteristicks,* by which the MESSIAH was to be distinguished from every other Person, do exactly agree in our Lord JESUS CHRIST, and in no other Person whatever."[31] The actual proof of this point involved detailed examination of Isaiah and other books of the Old Testament that seem to look forward to one who is to come who will have the government upon his shoulder.

The final and conclusive evidence, however, was the fact that Jesus and the apostles worked miracles. And they worked miracles, not merely out of compassion for suffering souls that sought healing, but in order to demonstrate that they were, in a very special sense, God's chosen instruments, whose word might be implicitly trusted. The argument was well stated by Thomas Barnard of Salem in 1768: "Not that I would be supposed to set up miracles as the only proof of it's truth. The excellency of the moral part of our religion—the agreement of what is merely revealed with our natural ideas of the holiness, mercy and sovereign wisdom of God—it's improving upon former dispensations of heaven—the accomplishment of ancient prophecies—the propagation of this cause in spite of all opposition. —All these and others are arguments of great weight. . . . [But] this of miracles is the capital proof in the case, which the founder of our faith laid the greatest stress upon. . . . For hereby he who delivered things worthy of God, proved that he came from God."[32]

To be sure, David Hume—whom Barnard described as "a subtle enemy of our faith"—had argued against miracles as a support for revelation. Even if miracles had actually occurred, Hume asserted, they are worthless as testimony because the chances for honest error or fraud on the part of witnesses are too great. But the supernatural rationalists were willing to accept even this challenge. Hume might undermine the claim for miracles in heathen religions; but the Christian miracles were different, for Christ performed them in such a way that there was no possibility that the witnesses were either deluded or deceivers. The miracles were performed publicly, not in obscure places; they were observed by hundreds of people who were possessed of common sense, if not of higher education; their reputations were such as they would not wish to jeopardize by being detected in falsehood; and there were even cases when they attested to their convictions by giving up their lives for them.

III

Here, then, are the essential principles of what we have called—for lack of a better name—"Supernatural Rationalism." Like the deists, the supernatural rationalists asserted the validity of Natural Religion, arguing for the existence of God largely in terms of a Creator who set the heavenly bodies moving harmoniously in their orbits. Unlike the deists, they also asserted the validity of Revealed Religion, which may present doctrines that are above reason, but not contrary to it. Like the deists, they assumed that acceptance of the claims of a particular religion to be a divine revelation is solely a matter of historical evidence and logical analysis. Unlike the deists—and skeptics like Hume—they were persuaded by the historical evidence for Christianity, especially the miracles. Other bases for Christian faith were set aside; its claims do not rest on religious experience, or on tradition, or on the authority of the Church, or on the witness of the Spirit, which had once assured the Puritan that the Bible was truly the Word of God.

When we speak in this way of the "supernatural rationalists," we should of course keep it in mind that we are not talking about a sect, or a denomination, or similar special group. The term refers to a position in a scheme of logical classification of ideas, not to a sociological entity. It is applied to theologians and preachers who hold a particular set of opinions, wherever they may be found. And they can be found in a variety of places, bearing many different labels, associated with more than one theological tradition. Supernatural Rationalism, as we have defined it, was not a complete theological system. It defined the basis for the acceptance of revelation, but it did not prescribe the content of that revelation. It declared that we are saved through the mediation of Christ, but did not prescribe how that mediation operated. Supernatural Rationalism never appeared by itself, but always in association with other doctrines; and it was differences over the doctrines of grace, rather than over the principles of rational religion, that divided orthodox from liberal, Calvinist from Arminian.

Here is an additional reason why scholars have so easily overlooked this kind of rationalism, and jumped to the conclusion that Deism was the typical form of rationalism in the eighteenth century. In the theological debates that went on over predestination, original sin, and the nature of justifying faith, the ground that Calvinist and Arminian held in common could be quickly passed over. It was only when the threat of infidelity, or Deism, seemed imminent that the rational defense of Revealed Religion came to the fore. Yet as soon as we become aware that the body of ideas we have called "Supernatural Rationalism" represents a well-defined tradition, we suddenly realize how all-pervasive it was. It can be found as early as 1700, and lingered well after 1850. It can be found in the writings of moderate Calvinists, and even some Edwardean Calvinists; it was well-nigh universal in the Arminian-Unitarian tradition; the Episcopalians took it for granted; Alexander Campbell impressed it on the Campbellite tradition; it had its spokesmen among the Presbyterians. The ideas of Supernatural Rationalism were disseminated so widely that it is impossible to map the field in detail without much more study than anyone has yet given to it. Doubtless, further exploration will reveal its presence in other groups than those just mentioned.

What is possible now, given the present state of our knowledge, is a few generalizations about the spread of these doctrines, together with some typical examples drawn from representatives of many different denominations. The generalizations are necessarily still tentative and incomplete. In the first place, Supernatural Rationalism and revivalism are uncongenial; and so one looks for it among opposers of the Great Awakening, rather than among strong supporters of it. In the second place, those religious groups in the colonies that were in close touch with British thought were particularly prone to adopt this kind of Christian apologetic. There is, actually, very little novelty in the colonial version of the doctrine. It tends to be an echo of British theology—of Tillotson, Locke, and Clarke in the beginning; of Butler and Lardner, among others, after mid-century; of George Campbell, Farmer, and Paley at a later date. Wherever these men and others of the same stamp were read and admired, the rationalist defense of Christianity against Deism was carried on with as much vigor as if Collins, Woolston, and Chubb had taken up residence in Boston or Philadelphia. This means that the Church of England was very largely influenced throughout the colonies, as well as a large element in the churches of the Standing Order in New England, the less revivalistic wing of the Presbyterian church, and, after the turn of the century, under the influence of Scottish theology, Alexander Campbell and the Campbellite movement.[33]

Early statements at least looking in the direction of Supernatural Rationalism may be found in the writings of both Increase and Cotton Mather. In 1700, the son published a tract called *Reasonable Religion;* and two years later, the father published *A Discourse Proving that the Christian Religion is the Only True Religion: wherein the Necessity of Divine Revelation is Evinced.* Increase Mather's tract is especially interesting because it represents a transitional position, and does not give up entirely the earlier doctrine that it is the witness of the Spirit in the heart of the reader that assures him that the Bible is the Word of God.[34] In 1712, Cotton Mather published *Reason Satisfied: and Faith Established,* which examined the historical evidence for the miracle of the resurrection, which was regarded as conclusive proof that Jesus Christ was a divinely inspired messenger. At about the same time, John Wise of Ipswich was summarizing the supernatural rationalist position in these words: "Revelation is Nature's Law in a fairer and brighter Edition."[35]

After the Great Awakening, the New England tradition divided in two, one half orthodox and Calvinist, the other liberal and Arminian. As we have already seen, the Dudleian lecturers were drawn from both sides of this division. Among the Calvinists, there were differences between the old or moderate Calvinists and the New Divinity men, followers of Edwards and Hopkins. At the outset it was moderate Calvinists who were especially susceptible to rationalism; but at the end of the century one finds Timothy Dwight, who was at least partly an heir of the Edwardean tradition, casting his five-volume systematic theology within the framework of Supernatural Rationalism. This treatise has a major division between a System of Doctrines and a System of Duties; and each major division is subdivided once more, the first part being based on Natural Religion, the second on the Christian revelation. In his treatment of miracles, Dwight rehearses the historical evidence in the familiar way, makes the usual reply to Hume, and declares that "the miracles of Christ are of vast importance, as proofs of the Divinity of his Mission."[36]

On the liberal or Arminian side of the line, this form of rationalism is no less prevalent.[37] In addition to the Dudleian lecturers we have previously encountered, one may note Jonathan Mayhew, who read and reread Lardner's *Credibility of the Gospel History;*[38] and William Bentley, whose Stone Chapel Sermon in 1790 referred to Natural Religion as "still the most excellent religion."[39] In our desire to make William Ellery Channing a prophet of Transcendentalism, we sometimes too easily overlook the fact that he too delivered a Dudleian lecture on *The Evidences of Revealed Religion,* in which he maintained that "Christianity is not only confirmed by miracles, but is in itself, in its very essence, a miraculous religion."[40]

Among Church of England divines in the colonies, Samuel Johnson gives an especially clear statement of Supernatural Rationalism. As early as 1727, he preached a sermon on "The Necessity of Revealed Religion," in which he acknowledged that "the light of nature has always discovered that there is a God," but then went on to point out what poor use the majority of men make of the reason that is theirs. Hence, "a divine and supernatural revelation, if such could be had, would certainly be the most compendious and expeditious method of bringing mankind in general to a just sense of God."[41]

Finally, the acceptance of these notions among Presbyterians in the middle colonies may be illustrated by excerpts from a series of presidents of Princeton. Thus Jonathan Dickinson published *The Reasonableness of Christianity, in Four Sermons,* in 1732. This was actually before the founding of Princeton, and Dickinson was at that time minister in Elizabeth-town, New Jersey. The first of Dickinson's four sermons was a demonstration of the being and attributes of God from the works of Creation. The second sermon demonstrates from rational argument, not from scripture, the depravity of human nature; the miserable circumstances of fallen man, the author states, make it appear most probable that the Christian revelation is true. Sermon three is a demonstration of the Christian religion from the prophecies of the Old Testament; while the final sermon is a demonstration of the Christian religion from the miracles wrought by our Lord Jesus Christ. The Newtonian flavor of Dickinson's discussion of Natural Religion comes out in the following passage particularly well:

> How came the parts of the *Earth* to cohere together, and not separately fly in the *boundless space?* Who has given the *Sea his decree,* bounded it by the shore, & said to its *proud waves, Hither shalt thou go and no further?* Who has hung the *Earth upon nothing,* and plac'd it in such due distance from the *Sun,* that it is neither by too near approaches to that *orb of Fire* scorch'd up and *consumed,* nor by a too remote station made a continent of *ice?* . . . Whence are those amazing & innumerable *Orbs* that *spangle* the *Sky,* plac'd and kept at due *distances,* and whirl'd in their several *courses,* without *interfering* and *dashing together* to the destruction of the World? Don't all these, and innumerable more *wonders of Nature* concur, to proclaim that man even mad as madness it self, that can suppose any lower *cause* of these things than *Infinite Wisdom?*[42]

Among Dickinson's successors as President of Princeton were Samuel Davies and John Witherspoon. The first sermon in Davies's collected works is one called "The Divine Authority and Sufficiency of the Christian Religion." This sermon is largely devoted to refuting the arguments of freethinkers on the subject of the miracles. The relationship between Natural Religion and Revealed Religion that Davies takes for granted is indicated in this sentence: "In the scriptures we find the faint discoveries of natural reason illustrated, its uncertain conjectures determined, and its mistakes corrected; so that Christianity includes natural religion in the greatest perfection."[43] Witherspoon's works, on the other hand, include a series of introductory lectures on Divinity, which he apparently delivered to students at Princeton who were planning to make the ministry their life work. Before discussing the typical doctrines of the reformed theology, such as the decrees, Witherspoon devoted eight lectures to Christian evidences, with special emphasis on the miracles, the fulfillment of prophecy, and the extraordinary spread of Christianity in the first three centuries.[44]

IV

These instances might be multiplied many times; but perhaps we have seen enough to recognize that here is a structure of ideas that has never been properly studied, at least in its American form, which was nevertheless a persistent concern of theologians and divines. It is a thing of the past, now, and has no power to stir us. Yet it once was the starting point of every young theological student's studies of divinity, as the biographies of Ezra Stiles and William Ellery Channing, among others, bear witness.

What happened to this structure of ideas? How did it pass from the scene after a long life of at least a century and a half? Emerson's Divinity School Address suggests at least part of the answer. Supernatural Rationalism was Christian apologetics, framed in language appropriate to the physics of Newton and the epistemology of Locke. When the Lockean philosophy lost its persuasiveness, Supernatural Rationalism became irrelevant. When Emerson began to utter a philosophy of intuition, and not of sensation, external evidences for Christianity, and the miracles in particular, suddenly seemed inconsequential. And when German Idealism took over the place that Scotch Realism had once filled as the reigning philosophy of the colleges and universities in this country, the disappearance of the older rationalism was almost as complete as the extinction of the passenger pigeon.

This particular kind of Christian apologetic has long since passed from the scene. But our image of the past lacks focus if we fail to recognize that for a century and a half it was as much taken for granted as the air men breathed. It would be an exaggeration to say that it was universally accepted; but it was certainly so widely accepted, across denominational lines, that one might justly call it the great ecumenical theology of its age. As such, the story of its rise and fall may be of interest to those among us who are concerned with the attempt to construct an ecumenical theology in our own day.

And its fate may also provide some sobering thoughts for any among you who may be turning over in your own minds the terms of an endowed lectureship you may be planning to establish for the perpetuation of your name to future generations.

THE REDISCOVERY OF CHANNING

I

We are well accustomed to strange and unaccountable fluctuations in the reputations of historical figures. Who would have supposed, in the year 1920, that the author of books about whaling and life in the South Seas would be regarded a generation later as one of the great masters of American literature? Who would have had any confidence in 1937, the centenary year of William Dean Howells, that he would begin to come into his own again, and be the subject for scholarly investigation on an increasing scale?

Sometimes the revival of interest in a neglected figure may be accounted for by the discovery of a mass of research material stored away in some forgotten attic, or by the release of such material, previously kept under restriction by the man himself or by his family. Thus the current editing of the Adams papers is giving impetus to new scholarly treatment of members of the Adams family. Sometimes a man's message may make more sense to one generation than it did to those preceding it—and so we rediscover Kierkegaard.

Considerations such as these do not seem to account for the recent rediscovery of Channing, however, and his changing reputation presents an especially puzzling problem. No large new masses of Channing papers have been found, and there is no reason to suppose that there are any to be discovered. If Channing has something to say to our generation, it is not because the Unitarians are calling that fact to our attention, as one might expect them to do. Yet the fact of an increase in the attention given to Channing by scholars is clear. Within the decade from 1952 to 1961, five full-length books dealing with aspects of his life and thought were published.[1] The biography by John White Chadwick, printed in 1903, had been the last previous book of any consequence. These recent books are not isolated phenomena. There must also be mentioned a series of scholarly articles, beginning in 1929, and at least three dissertations that have not been published, even in part.[2]

Since no significant new information about Channing has been uncovered, the problem posed by this recent Channing scholarship is essentially one of interpretation of familiar material. In this connection, it seems to me that there has been a growing tendency to give currency to certain misconceptions about Channing's intellectual background, his theological position, and his relationship to his younger contemporaries. More specifically, it appears that the influence of Samuel Hopkins on Channing in his early years has been misinterpreted and vastly exaggerated, while the tendency towards Transcendentalism in the later years has been magnified to an unwarranted degree. These matters of interpretation are sufficiently important to receive detailed consideration.

II

The question of Channing's intellectual background has been discussed by the authors of several of the books and articles under review, who, with various degrees of explicitness, suggest that Samuel Hopkins was a major formative influence. Thus Professor Herbert W. Schneider has argued that three separate faiths or systems of thought prevailed in revolutionary New England: rationalism, pietism, and republicanism. Channing inherited all three, according to Schneider, and his thought is to some extent a synthesis of them all. "Pietism" here has a very special meaning. It does not merely designate a tradition in which religion is regarded as an affair of the heart or the emotions, and Christian experience is to be emphasized at least as much as Christian doctrine. In that sense, Channing may certainly be looked upon as a combination of pietism and rationalism. Professor Schneider's use of the term, however, is much more restricted. "I shall use pietism," he explains, "as a synonym for Edwardeanism and the New Light movement." It is in this sense that we are to understand his assertion that "Channing's early life and thought were dominated by a pietistic environment."

Newport in Channing's boyhood, he asserts, "was dominated theologically by Samuel Hopkins, the champion of 'consistent Calvinism.' "[3]

At one point in his article, Professor Schneider acknowledges that Channing's early impressions of Hopkins were unfavorable, but he nevertheless assumes that his theological bent was originally set by the prevailing influence of the Newport minister. When he comes to discuss the influence of Hutcheson and Ferguson on Channing, therefore, he introduces a quotation from Ferguson with these words: "Imagine the effect of the following sentences on a young mind steeped in Edwardean theology." Towards the close of the article, Channing's reaction to Theodore Parker's rejection of miracles is presented as "one further illustration of Channing's faithfulness to his early pietism."[4] In short, here is an account of Channing's intellectual development which asserts that the earliest influences on him were Hopkinsian, that he went to Harvard College as a Hopkinsian, and that traces of Hopkinsianism remained with him throughout his career.[5]

Professor Schneider's article was published in 1938, and scholars who have worked on Channing since that time have repeated this interpretation with varying degrees of emphasis. Professor Robert Leet Patterson in 1952 referred to Hopkins as "a living link between Edwards and Channing"; he argued that while Channing ultimately rejected Calvinism as repulsive, in the early days of his ministry "he was prepared to swallow all these dogmas."[6] More recently, David Edgell's book on Channing continues this line of interpretation. At one point it refers to the "distance between Channing's Christianity and that of Hopkins out of which it grew." Elsewhere it asserts that "Channing's own revolution was a continuance of the Hopkinsian revolt." After a description of an early so-called conversion or "change of heart" on Channing's part, Edgell says: "Here, it seems to me, is an orthodox account of an orthodox conversion." He also declares that there is "abundant evidence" that as late as 1809 "the public thought of him as an orthodox Hopkinsian, if not an orthodox Calvinist."[7]

These claims for the influence of Hopkins on Channing go far beyond anything that is to be found in the earlier biographies by William Henry Channing or John White Chadwick. They represent a recent trend in Channing scholarship, and one that has developed, it seems to me, from a very serious misreading of the historical record. The source of the misinterpretation may well be chiefly Professor

Schneider's article, which has never been subjected to careful examination, so that later writers have tended to echo it uncritically. To set the record straight, a review of the early decades of Channing's life is required.

Channing was born in Newport in 1780. There were then two congregational churches in the town, the First Church, of which Hopkins had been minister since 1770, and the Second, where Ezra Stiles had been installed in 1755. Both men had been forced to abandon their charges during the British occupation, which left the two churches in an enfeebled condition. Stiles did not return to Newport after the war, but accepted the presidency of Yale College in 1778. Hopkins came back in 1780 to find only a handful of his flock remaining.

The Channing family were members of the Second Church, and it was Stiles who baptized young William during a two-week visit to his former parish. The pulpit of the Second Church remained vacant until 1786, however, and during the intervening period the Channing family went to Hopkins's church. The inadequacies of Hopkins's preaching were notorious, and Channing was repulsed by them as a child. "My first impressions were not very favorable," he declared long afterwards. "I can distinctly recollect, that the prevalence of terror in his preaching was a very common subject of remark, and gave rise to ludicrous stories among the boys."[8] In view of the small size of Hopkins's congregation and the quality of his preaching, one may well doubt whether Newport was "dominated theologically" by him. Certainly the Channing family could not have been much attracted, for as soon as William Patten came to fill Ezra Stiles's old pulpit, they returned to the Second Church. The influence of Stiles continued to be felt in the Channing household, and Channing went so far as to declare, in later life, that in his earliest years he regarded "no human being with equal reverence."[9] Stiles was a moderate Calvinist, but he stood for private judgment, tolerance, and cooperation among all Christians regardless of theological differences. It was presumably moderate Calvinism of the Stiles variety, rather than Hopkinsianism that was the theological atmosphere of Channing's early Newport days.

From the age of twelve to the age of fourteen, Channing lived with his uncle, the Reverend Henry Channing of New London. Lacking clear evidence from printed sermons, we cannot pin down Henry Channing's theological views with any precision. It is suggestive, however,

that at a later date he left his pulpit, following an episode in which
he was sharply criticized for rather too enthusiastic support of the Reverend John Sherman of Mansfield, Connecticut. It was Sherman who
got into trouble in 1805 because of an antitrinitarian tract entitled
One God in One Person Only. There is no way to prove conclusively
that Henry Channing was an out-and-out Arminian in the years 1792
to 1794, let alone an antitrinitarian, but local historians and the authors
of biographical sketches have agreed that he was at least tending in that
direction, perhaps from the very beginning of his ministry.[10]

From the age of fourteen to the age of eighteen, Channing was at
Harvard, a member of the class of 1798. The Harvard influence could
have been anything from moderate Calvinism to Arminianism. President Joseph Willard and Professor David Tappan were Calvinists;
John Pierce, Channing's tutor, tended towards Arminianism and ultimately became an avowed Unitarian. There were no Hopkinsians in
Cambridge. It should be recalled that the line between the moderate
Calvinist and the Arminian was often hard to distinguish at that time.
In theory, the Calvinists believed in the eternal decrees, while the Arminians did not, but both groups declared that man was in need of
redemption by God's grace, and as long as they stuck to that common
theme, it was hard to tell them apart. There is no evidence by which
Channing can clearly be designated as belonging in his undergraduate
days to one rather than the other of the two groups.

His reading, however, was strangely lacking in evangelical and orthodox writers. Judging by the charging lists of the college library, the
closest he came to orthodoxy was when he took out Watts's *Essays*
towards the end of his sophomore year. Nothing by Edwards or Hopkins seems to have attracted him. Instead he was reading English and
Scottish writers, of a rationalistic and even at times a Socinian temper.
The list includes John Leland, Thomas Belsham, Joseph Priestley, and
even David Hume, although conceivably Hume was read for purposes
of refutation. Richard Price is on the list, and from him Channing
learned that the sensational psychology of Locke did not have to end
in the skepticism of Hume. A similar lesson was found in Thomas
Reid. Other representatives of the Scottish school whose books were
especially important to Channing were Hutcheson and Ferguson; the
impact on him of his reading of Hutcheson under the willows is a familiar part of the Channing biography. The library charging lists

which enable us to verify this course of reading, it is reassuring to note, indicate at the bottom of the page: "All retd in gd order."[11]

It was while at Harvard that Channing's vocational bent finally turned away from law or medicine to the ministry. First of all, however, he had to review for himself the traditional evidences of the Christian revelation. The pattern of the argument that satisfied him was commonplace among the liberals of his day, and familiar enough to the moderate Calvinists. It was perhaps less typical of the consistent Calvinists or Edwardeans.[12]

After graduation, Channing spent eighteen months as a tutor in Virginia, in the Randolph family. This experience had an unsettling effect on his political views, but his theological tendencies were confirmed rather than altered. He continued to read history, especially Hume and Ferguson; in philosophy he spoke at this time with particular enthusiasm of Priestley and Ferguson. A letter printed in the *Memoir* gives an account of the sequence of theological studies he pursued, beginning with Christian evidences, and moving thence to Christian doctrine based on the Bible apart from polemical divinity and the creeds.[13] This letter so perfectly states the liberal or Arminian approach, particularly in its concern lest the doctrines of the Bible be contaminated by man-made systems of divinity, that it is hard to believe that its author was even a moderate Calvinist. His reference at the time to a "conversion" or "change of heart" scarcely alters the picture, since Arminians had not yet abandoned the traditional concern for an inward regeneration, even though they rejected unconditional election and eschewed revivalistic methods. Channing's Richmond sojourn reveals him to have been emotional in temper, emphasizing a religion of the heart as much as any evangelical ever did, but at the same time avoiding the doctrines that were regarded as distinctively evangelical.

When Channing returned to Newport in 1800, he was twenty years old, and there is little reason to doubt that the tendency of his thinking was already established. What the evidence suggests is a position wholly consistent with the liberal Christianity of that date. It fits somewhat less well with moderate Calvinism; it contains not a hint of the peculiarities of the Hopkinsian system, such as the willingness to be damned for the glory of God, the depreciation of the use of means in salvation, or the assertion that sin exists by divine permission.

It was at this point in his development that Channing became acquainted with Hopkins. He found that Hopkins was not the embodiment of gloom and despair that he had supposed from his childhood experience; he found much to admire and praise in the older man, and he reached the conclusion that he was much misunderstood, by his followers as well as by his opponents. Yet it must not be overlooked that what attracted him to Hopkins was one aspect of Hopkins's system only, the concept of disinterested benevolence. The system as a whole did not appeal to him, and he drew on Hopkins very selectively for those things for which his reading of Hutcheson had prepared him. Professor Schneider's assumption that Hutcheson and Ferguson appealed to him because he was steeped in Hopkinsianism from childhood is not merely incorrect; it is an exact inversion of the true sequence of events. The evidence may be presented in Channing's own words: "I had studied with great delight during my college life the philosophy of Hutcheson, and the Stoical morality, and these had prepared me for the noble, self-sacrificing doctrines of Dr. Hopkins."[14] In the Newport sermon of 1836, in which he paid tribute to Hopkins, it is noteworthy that he was discriminating and selective in his comments. Benevolence was the significant thing he found in Hopkins, and even Hopkins's concept of benevolence in Channing's hands was developed in a non-Edwardean way.

III

The notion of Hopkins as a major creative influence on Channing in his early years must clearly be abandoned. Though Hopkins influenced him at one point in a very specific way, the Hopkinsian tradition was not his chief nourishment, nor were any Hopkinsians, apart from Hopkins himself, at any time intimates of his. Yet even if we acknowledge that Channing was no Hopkinsian, the question remains whether he was a Calvinist in the early years of his ministry, and therefore to be ranked among the orthodox rather than among the liberal Christians. Because there was an "evangelical" zeal and fervor in his preaching, it is argued that he must also have adhered to orthodox doctrine. Besides, so the argument runs, in 1808 John Codman invited him to preach at his ordination. Codman's Calvinism was most explicitly avowed; Codman would not have invited a Unitarian to preach for him and a Unitarian would not have accepted; and, finally, the sermon Channing preached was Calvinistic in its depiction of the awful penalties of wickedness.

Actually, the bare fact of Channing's participation in Codman's ordination proves little, since the ordaining council was made up of both liberals and orthodox, and several of the men who took part in the service itself were unmistakably liberals. Joseph Stevens Buckminster gave the introductory prayer; Thaddeus Mason Harris was assigned the right hand of fellowship; and Charles Lowell gave the concluding prayer. These men were representative of the liberal Christians of that day. To be sure, they were not avowed Unitarians, since none of the liberals at that time would accept that designation, save only James Freeman, whose situation was peculiar because he was minister of the Stone Chapel, and not one of the congregational churches. Party lines were beginning to tighten; but the process had not yet gone so far as to prevent common participation in an ordination service.

Channing's early preaching in general, however, and this sermon in particular have frequently been characterized as Calvinistic. Thus Joshua Bates recalled that in his early years Channing preached with solemnity and directness of application "on the guilt of sin, the depravity of human nature, the danger of impenitent sinners, the holiness and spirituality of the divine law, the glories of the divine character, and the riches of redeeming grace." Bates, who was a friend and supporter of Codman in the controversy that soon broke out in the Dorchester church, went on to intimate that Channing's power as a preacher declined in later years in proportion as he emerged as a leader of the new Unitarian group.[15]

Yet the evidence is clear that as early as 1806 Channing regarded himself as belonging among the liberal Christians, and not among the orthodox. In the spring of that year, he was corresponding with his grandfather, William Ellery, who still defended Calvinistic doctrine. Two letters survive in which Channing attempts to expound, if not the doctrines of the liberal Christians, at least the spirit that informed them. In March, 1806, he wrote: "You will see from this that our standard of divinity does not entirely correspond with yours. It is clear that we cannot all be right." He then urges, in good liberal fashion, that men should be judged by the state of their hearts, rather than by the orthodoxy of their doctrines. Evidently the grandfather wrote back, repeating the familiar complaint of the orthodox that the liberals were slurring over essential doctrines of the reformed theology, for Channing replied: "You complain that our standard is not *particular* enough. But this is the distinguishing feature of our system of liberality. The greater the variety of sentiments with which a system will harmonize, or the fewer its fundamentals, the more worthy it is of liberal minds."

A year later, the discussion was still unfinished. Mr. Ellery insisted that it is necessary to "entertain just ideas of the moral attributes of God, of the depravity of man, of the atonement of Christ, and the influence of the Holy Spirit." Channing's reply was that just ideas on these points are doubtless necessary, but our ignorance is such that we cannot insist on a single rigid standard of doctrinal truth. "With respect to the depravity of man," he wrote, "I think it important that it should be most deeply and painfully felt. . . . But while I acknowledge this, I am by no means ready to say that no man can be a Christian who does not believe in the total depravity of human nature. A man may doubt on that subject, yet hate sin."[16] Channing's distinction here between "the depravity of man" and "the total depravity of human nature," one suspects, is not accidental.

The Codman ordination sermon, then, was preached by a young man who had already associated himself with the liberal Christians. Read in this perspective, it becomes a fascinating example of the way in which traditional Calvinist doctrines could be skirted or suppressed by the early liberals, and at the same time an evangelical temper be communicated to the congregation. Channing was temperamentally inclined towards this kind of accommodation, but he doubtless had good reason to seek it, since both liberals and orthodox were to be found within his own congregation. His preaching had quickly attracted hearers from other churches, including some who moved over in the summer of 1803 from the Old South Church.[17] For at least a decade after his own ordination, his way of ministering to a somewhat mixed congregation involved an evangelical, almost pietistic style of preaching, combined with a refusal to touch on the "peculiar doctrines" of Calvinism.

The early liberals were often accused of concealing their real position; Channing's sermon suggests one of the ways by which this was done. By the standards of a later generation, as John White Chadwick's biography gives witness, this sermon was not merely orthodox, it was "hyper-orthodox." But standards of orthodoxy change; and what we sometimes forget is that a somber view of human nature and human destiny was common among the liberals at the time of the Codman ordination, and, indeed, for some time thereafter. These men rejected the decrees, and denied that we are punished in any sense for the guilt of Adam's sin. But they freely acknowledged the actual and universal sinfulness of men, which they found to be imperfectly controlled by inner strivings after righteousness. They fully expected that appropriate punishment would be inflicted by God on sinful men, even while they argued that punishment was for discipline and correction, so that unruly hearts would ultimately be subdued. Admittedly, in his Codman sermon Channing referred to the "fire which is never quenched" and the "worm which never dies." But so did Henry Ware, Sr., as late as 1842, long after most Unitarians were speaking another theological language entirely.[18]

At this stage in his theological development, Channing had not yet developed his later outspoken antipathy to Calvinism as unfavorable to piety. But he had already decided against the doctrine of the Trinity, and was firm in his opposition to the exclusive policy that was increasingly characteristic of the orthodox faction, under the leadership of Jedidiah Morse. He was notably reluctant to see theological parties form and was, therefore, unwilling to press differences to the point of separation. Hence his contemporaries had some difficulty in knowing how to categorize him. His parishioner Thomas Dawes heard him speak favorably of Moses Stuart in 1809, his remarks seeming to indicate agreement on predestination and free will. But Dawes immediately acknowledged that in his preaching Channing "never touches those dreadful points."[19] That same year, when the Park Street Church was organized in order to provide a bastion of orthodoxy amid the creeping liberalism of the Boston churches, the Federal Street Church was invited to send delegates; but the invitation was declined on the grounds that the basis for it was narrow and exclusive. The comment of John Pierce, the minister in Brookline and Channing's old tutor, is a revealing one:

> Why they should choose Mr Channing as one, it is not easy to conceive, as he has always manifested his doubts, if not disbelief of the doctrine of the Trinity, which one of their leaders [Dr. Morse] has often been heard to declare "the splitting point." It might possibly be with the

hope of bringing over to their side, one, who appears to favour them in so many other respects, one who would be a great acquisition to any cause. But he was not to be so easily inclined to commit himself.[20]

The Codman ordination sermon was, of course, in no sense an exposition of theological doctrine, whether liberal, moderate Calvinist, or Hopkinsian. Doctrinal statements in it were incidental to the main purpose, which was to urge the young minister to approach his tasks with fervent zeal. The concept of religion expressed is one that stresses emotional fervor, but not systematic or dogmatic theology. This aspect of the sermon readily won the applause of liberals. Henry Ware, Jr., read it in 1813, and wrote with enthusiasm to his father about it. "It seems to me powerful and impressive beyond example," he declared. "It must be a treasure to young ministers, and ought to stop effectually the cold sermonizing of your rationalists, who maintain the strange contradiction, of religion without feeling."[21]

The elder Henry Ware took the remark, as perhaps it was intended, as an implied criticism of the liberal preachers of his own generation. "I do not know," he wrote back, "exactly what you mean by the cold rationalists, who maintain religion without feeling. Never, perhaps, was a charge more unjustly applied than that usually is." For his part, he regarded Channing's sermon as "one of the happiest efforts of pulpit eloquence," and Channing himself as a living refutation of the notion that warmth and zeal in religion cannot coexist with enlightened doctrine. "The thing itself which you mean to censure," he went on to say, "I most heartily join with you in censuring; but you will find that coldness is not exclusively the attribute of the rational. You will find that the irrational may also be cold and heartless."[22]

The Codman ordination sermon, however, is not the only utterance by Channing that has been adduced to support the notion that he was essentially orthodox. On one occasion, Channing described his own spiritual progress in these words, which seem to refer to a period prior to his ordination: "There was a time when I verged towards Calvinism, for ill health and depression gave me a dark view of things. But the doctrine of the Trinity held me back."[23] It is an amusing commentary on the use of evidence that William Henry Channing used this passage in the *Memoir* as conclusive proof that his uncle never was orthodox. The crucial point here is, of course, the use of the word "Calvinism."

What did Channing mean by it in this context? It may well be that the "argument from tendency" used by Channing in his later attacks on Calvinism, and particularly in "The Moral Argument Against Calvinism," influenced his choice of words. The argument from tendency, briefly stated, is that Calvinism *tends* to encourage a contracted, gloomy, pessimistic view of things, and that this psychological consequence of accepting Calvinistic doctrine is enough to condemn it. The word "Calvinism" thus becomes a symbol for a gloomy outlook on life, rather than a specific set of doctrines.

The clearest statement by Channing himself of his own spiritual and intellectual growth, however, has frequently been overlooked in discussions of this matter. It is to be found in a letter written in 1840 to a young man searching for religious truth. His inquiries into religion, he explained, "grew out of the shock given to my moral nature by the popular system of faith which I found prevailing round me in my early years. All my convictions of justice and goodness revolted against the merciless dogmas then commonly taught." He turned to the Scriptures, where he learned that Christ came into the world to save men from impurity and moral evil, not from punishment, and that God imparts his strength and light to every man who strives for perfection and the conquest of evil. "You will easily see," he concluded, "how these views scattered all the darkness into which I had been plunged by a false, traditional faith."[24]

In summary, the earliest religious influences on Channing were those of moderate Calvinism. While at Harvard, and possibly even earlier, he became familiar with a more liberal theology. His study of the Scriptures while in Virginia confirmed him in his new views. The influence of Hopkins was a later and very selective thing, which reinforced his established tendency to define morality in terms of benevolence. Like the other liberal Christians, he was reluctant to stress issues that would lead to divisions within the churches; yet there is no doubt where his sympathies lay. From the day when he read Hutcheson under the willows in Cambridge, while an undergraduate, to the day more than two decades later when he preached for an hour and a half at Jared Sparks's ordination, there was development and increased resoluteness in the statement of his religious views, but no change in direction, for the bent of his career was already fixed.

IV

If Channing's early career has been misrepresented to make it appear that he was really a Hopkinsian, his later career has been misrepresented in a different direction to make it appear that he was a Transcendentalist, or virtually such. David Edgell's book may serve to illustrate this tendency in recent scholarship also. To be sure, Edgell can find only a few utterances, such as the ordination sermon entitled "Likeness to God," that seem to him clearly transcendentalist, but he devotes a whole chapter to tracing similarities between Channing and Emerson and the other Transcendentalists. By the time he is through, his preliminary qualifications and doubts have disappeared, and he bluntly asserts:

> The whole tenor of his later life shows a Transcendental bias. That his disagreements with Emerson, Alcott, and Parker were many is not important, for all the Transcendentalists disagreed among themselves: disagreement was almost an article of faith. That there were philosophical differences from a strict philosophical definition of Transcendentalism is equally true and equally unimportant, for American Transcendentalism was literary and romantic rather than philosophical in character. Among Unitarians, one may ask, does Channing belong with Norton or Parker?[25]

Whether Channing belongs with Norton or with Parker is an interesting question, and I suspect the answer is not so obvious as some might suppose. If on the other hand one alters the question to read: Among Unitarians does Channing belong with Henry Ware, Jr., or with Parker? the answer is clear. He belongs with the younger Henry Ware, whom no one ever accused of being a Transcendentalist. The real question, however, must not be lost among the rhetorical ones. The real question is how we distinguish a transcendentalist Unitarian from the other kind, and which category applies in this particular case.

This is a problem that has proved a bothersome one in American intellectual history, and Channing is not the only man about whom some question has arisen. Of Theodore Parker himself, Professor Schneider has remarked that he was a Transcendentalist "only to a very limited degree," while John Edward Dirks has reached the conclusion that he "stood near, but not within, New England transcendentalism."

On the other hand, H. Shelton Smith has reviewed the evidence and reached the conclusion that "traditional scholarship has not been essentially wrong in placing Parker within that circle of left-wing religious thinkers."[26] George Ripley's credentials as a member of the group were examined some time ago by Arthur R. Schultz and Henry A. Pochman in an article entitled: "George Ripley: Unitarian, Transcendentalist, or Infidel?" The authors agreed that he was not an infidel, but were nonplussed as to what he really was. "About all that can be said," they reported by way of conclusion, "is that he was never between 1820 and 1850 a Unitarian of Norton's kind nor a Transcendentalist of Parker's sort."[27] This conclusion may well be sound, but it is not very helpful. If many more such articles are written, there will be no Transcendentalists left.

Edgell's attempt to stress the transcendentalist element in Channing actually revives an older tradition in literary scholarship. When Arthur I. Ladu reviewed the problem in 1939 in his article on "Channing and Transcendentalism," he was able to cite half a dozen books and articles in which Channing was presented either as a Transcendentalist or as a precursor of Transcendentalism. One of the most explicit of such interpretations may be found in Goddard's *Studies in New England Transcendentalism* (1908): "all those distinctive doctrines which gave his preaching uniqueness and significance in his own day and which give him historical importance now, flowed from the transcendental elements in his belief."[28] Ladu's article, however, reaches the opposite conclusion: "As cultivated men of religious and philosophical temperament, the transcendentalists and Channing had various common interests, and they appear generally to have admired one another. But their philosophies were not in accord. Channing was interested solely in a purer Christianity. He was not a transcendentalist."[29]

There are two possible approaches to the problem of whether Channing, or indeed any one of his contemporaries, was a Transcendentalist. On the one hand, one might think of the Transcendentalists as a more or less self-conscious group, who engaged in common activities and turned to one another for support and stimulus. This approach would emphasize the list of participants in the so-called Transcendental Club, the promoters of the *Dial,* and perhaps the inhabitants of Brook Farm. Alternatively, one may think of the Transcendentalists as sharing a particular point of view on some important issue or principle in religion or philosophy. Where they stood may be gleaned from sermons or lectures, but sometimes their reaction to a significant occasion, such as Emerson's Divinity School address, is enough to reveal their allegiance.

The first of these approaches is moderately helpful, though not without difficulties, especially with such an unsocial person as Channing. There are other anomalies as well. What of Nathaniel Langdon Frothingham, who was invited to attend the Transcendental Club, and whom Emerson mentioned warmly and approvingly in his Journal? What of Nathaniel Hawthorne, who actually lived at Brook Farm? It would be absurd to include them, and we know better than to do so. The difficulty is that most of the leading Transcendentalists were Unitarian ministers, who necessarily interacted with one another anyway. The group always remained a rather amorphous element within the larger body and never developed the kind of cohesion that would enable us to define it precisely as a sociological entity. It is actually much easier to use patterns of interaction to distinguish a Calvinist from a liberal Christian at the beginning of Channing's career than to use them to distinguish a Transcendentalist from one of the more conservative Unitarians at the end of it.

For this reason, it is usually considered much more revealing to try to define a philosophical or theological difference between the conservative Unitarian and the transcendentalist Unitarian. Two quotations point the way. One is from a letter of Emerson to his brother Edward in 1834:

> . . . do you draw the distinction of Milton Coleridge & the Germans between Reason & Understanding. I think it a philosophy itself. . . . Reason is the highest faculty of the soul—what we mean often by the soul itself; it never *reasons,* never proves, it simply perceives; it is vision. The Understanding toils all the time, compares, contrives, adds, argues, near sighted but strong-sighted, dwelling in the present the expedient the customary. . . . Reason is potentially perfect in every man—Understanding in very different degrees of strength. . . . The manifold applications of the distinction to Literature to the Church to Life will show how good a key it is.[30]

The second quotation is from the diary of Convers Francis, in 1836. "I have long seen," he wrote, "that the Unitarians must break into two schools,—the Old one, or English school, belonging to the sensual and empiric philosophy,—and the New one, or the German school (perhaps it may be called), belonging to the spiritual philosophy."[31]

These passages are enough to remind us that what fired the young men who became Transcendentalists in the 1830s and 1840s was the discovery that there was an alternative philosophy to that of Locke and the Lockean tradition. For more than a century, the accepted philosophy in New England was based on the sensational psychology of Locke or else the modified Lockeanism of the Scotch Realists. The time had long since passed when one fell on Locke with a sense of novelty and new discovery, as Edwards had once done. Now the Lockean tradition was thoroughly orthodox and established, and its spokesmen acted as though all philosophical questions had at last been answered. The young rebels went to the root of this philosophical orthodoxy, and insisted that there is another source of knowledge besides sensation and reflection. There is a direct intuition of religious and moral truths which is of a higher order than the worldly Understanding, "that wrinkled calculator the steward of our house to whom is committed the support of our animal life."[32]

Both Mr. Ladu in his article on "Channing and the Transcendentalists" and Mr. Smith in his on Theodore Parker quite legitimately make adherence to an intuitional theory of knowledge the touchstone of Transcendentalism. "Insistence upon the validity of immediate intuition, independent of any external experience or teaching, is an important tenet in the transcendental philosophy," says Mr. Ladu.[33] Professor Smith's position is similar: "the new Unitarian transcendentalists subscribed, in varying degrees, to the doctrine of the direct or immediate perception of religious truth. . . . Thus they explicitly rejected the Lockean idea that all knowledge springs out of sensory experience."[34] If we accept this as a proper test of what makes a Transcendentalist, it is clear that Channing does not qualify. As late as the time of Parker's South Boston sermon, Channing was reiterating that the truth of Christianity depends on the historical evidence for the miracles of Christ. Only on Lockean principles can this intense concern for the miracles as Christian evidences be understood. For adherents of the intuitional school, the argument for Christianity in terms of the historical miracles had long since shriveled into triviality.

The detailed evidence that Channing was no Transcendentalist, in the sense of an adherent of the intuitional philosophy, has been well rehearsed by Mr. Ladu and need not be repeated here. If one keeps in mind Channing's concept of God as personality, and of man's likeness to God as the essential similarity of one distinct personality to another, the sermon "Likeness to God" does not sound quite so transcendental as some readers have thought. Channing believed that men are like their Creator in much the same way that a child bears a resemblance to his father, except that the qualities of men are finite and imperfect while those of God are infinite. "And what is it to be a Father?" Channing asked. "It is to communicate one's own nature, to give life to kindred beings; and the highest function of a Father is to educate the mind of the child, and to impart to it what is noblest and happiest in his own mind."[35] This is a very different thing from the transcendentalist concept of the divine influx of the Oversoul into the souls of men, or Emerson's transparent eyeball.

V

A final question remains. Why is it that scholars seem to have a persistent urge to identify Channing with Transcendentalism, and to minimize the points he held in common with the more conservative Unitarians of his time? Why is it that, two generations ago, Professor Harold C. Goddard insisted that "he was scarcely a Unitarian at all"?[36] Why is it that whenever Mr. Edgell finds a parallel between Channing and Emerson he assumes that Channing is essentially a Transcendentalist, and does not explore the possibility that Emerson may retain many of the attitudes and values of the earlier Unitarianism that nurtured him? The answer seems to be that Channing has been treated chiefly by historians of American letters, rather than historians of American religious ideas. Our literary historians know of Transcendentalism directly, in their reading of Emerson and Thoreau, but they are concerned with the Unitarianism from which it sprang chiefly for its bearing on later literary movements. Channing attracts their attention because, though not a Transcendentalist, he was the patron saint of the Transcendentalists. They come to Channing with special concerns, and find in him what is most relevant to their special interests.

They also come to him with a very inadequate knowledge of the Unitarianism of Channing's contemporaries. The impression that seems to prevail of the faith of the early Unitarians is that it was a desiccated structure of theological negations without heart or flesh. Thus a recent historian of American letters refers to it as "a rather pale, formal faith."[37] And two authors of a handbook to be used in courses on American literature declare:

> As originally formulated, Unitarianism was dry and rationalistic in the extreme. It had little concept of religion as a deeply felt psychological experience, and attempted to approximate the spirit of scientific inquiry in its approach to the Bible as the word of God.[38]

The source of this image of Unitarianism is not hard to find. Two men were perhaps more responsible for it than anyone else. One of them was Emerson, whose references to "the pale negations of Boston Unitarianism" and "the corpse-cold Unitarianism of Brattle Street" have seemed to lovers of picturesque phraseology to be an adequate characterization of the faith of Channing's generation, and to make firsthand investigation of the record of that generation unnecessary. The other was Octavius Brooks Frothingham, whose biography of his father, entitled *Boston Unitarianism*, has often been taken as a basis for wholesale generalization. Frothingham's own spiritual progress involved a phase of sharp reaction against the values for which his father stood; and mingled with a sense of obligation to do justice to the memory of his father, his book contains a residue of the basic lack of sympathy between the generations. Furthermore, the author declared that he was characterizing but one kind of Unitarian of the early period. There were three kinds in all, he stated, and he hoped to recover from oblivion a forgotten and neglected type. No one would perhaps have been more surprised than he to realize how readily his description of one kind of Unitarian would be accepted as representative of the whole movement.

Naturally, if one starts with a stereotype of the kind we have noted, a problem arises as soon as one reads Channing. He fails to fit the preconceived image. The immediate reaction seems to be: evidently Channing was not really a Unitarian, or at any rate, was a most atypical one. Before long it develops that he was a Hopkinsian in his youth and a Transcendentalist in his later years, and his Unitarianism is set aside because no one knows quite how to deal with it. The Supernatural Rationalism of Channing's Dudleian Lecture, which is central to an understanding of his theology, is overlooked. Here is a man who has been discussed in terms of one part of the past that he inherited, and in terms of the future he influenced, but most inadequately in terms of the present in which he lived.

The judgment passed by a rebellious younger generation on the achievement of its fathers is always partial and incomplete, and so the testimony we have accepted from the Transcendentalists regarding the faith of the early Unitarians needs to be supplemented. And I rather suspect that if we start looking around, and read the neglected biography of Henry Ware, Jr., and the writings of Orville Dewey; if we recall Joseph Stevens Buckminster, John Emery Abbot, Nathan Parker, and Joseph Tuckerman; and perhaps even if we try to reexamine the work of Andrews Norton with a fresh, unbiased eye, we shall discover a richer and more varied picture than we had thought, and find that Channing was not alone in seeking a living religion that would stir the hearts of men, rather than a formal and conventional one of externals only.

EMERSON, BARZILLAI FROST, AND THE
DIVINITY SCHOOL ADDRESS

The Reverend Barzillai Frost, minister of the Unitarian church in Concord from 1837 to 1857, does not loom large in the biographies of Emerson. Cabot does not even mention him; Rusk refers to him but once. His name seldom appears in the Journals, and in the published letters there are only a few unimportant allusions to him.

Yet there is clear evidence that Frost greatly affected Emerson at a critical juncture in the latter's career, that it was because of Emerson's reaction to Frost's preaching that the Divinity School Address took the shape and color that it did. Because Emerson named no names in that Address, it has been taken at face value as a general and presumably just criticism of the dead and formal preaching of the day. It has not been appreciated that crucial passages of it were originally specific criticisms of one particular minister, later generalized and made anonymous for a public occasion. But once that fact is made clear, and the relationship between Emerson and his own minister has been probed, a wholly new dimension is added to our understanding of the Address.

I propose, therefore, to reconstruct the origin and gestation of the Divinity School Address in the living context of Emerson's experiences in pulpit and pew, Sunday after Sunday, in 1837 and 1838. The result may well be a new perspective on the state of religion and the churches at that time, a clearer picture of Emerson's methods of literary composition, and above all a greater awareness of the importance of the Address in the spiritual biography of its author.

I

On Wednesday, the first day of February 1837, the Reverend Barzillai Frost was ordained by the church in Concord, and installed as colleague to the aged Dr. Ezra Ripley. Ralph Waldo Emerson was present, and seated next to him during a part of the proceedings was the Reverend Caleb Stetson, who had ridden over from Medford to deliver the "Address to the Society." Stetson was a member of the group that had begun to meet from time to time as "Hedge's Club," or the "Transcendental Club." During the ordination ceremonies, he kept whispering witticisms to Emerson, who found it difficult to maintain an appropriately dignified demeanor.[1]

The most impressive part of the ordination service was the Charge, delivered by the Reverend Henry Ware, Jr. Ware had been Emerson's predecessor as minister of the Second Church in Boston. In 1829, ill health had forced him to give up his pulpit and to accept instead a professorship of pastoral care at the Divinity School in Cambridge. Of the Unitarian ministers in and around Boston, he was second only to Dr. Channing in popular esteem. He was regarded as an eloquent and moving preacher, though perhaps not quite so polished as Channing, and he was conspicuously successful in the pastoral care of his flock. The Unitarians of that generation thought of him as the ideal type of the parish minister, whose accomplishments were a living example of the possibilities for good which the office of the minister afforded.[2]

To the students at the Divinity School, Ware was a spiritual counselor and friend, quite as much as a teacher. No one was ever more beloved by his students than he, and they almost always asked him—as Barzillai Frost did—to participate in their ordinations. His concept of religion was deeply emotional, and he communicated to his hearers some sense of his own piety. His Charge to Frost was a threefold injunction: to be diligent in business, fervent in spirit, serving the Lord, "these three, industry, enthusiasm, and piety,—but the greatest of these is PIETY." Of this Charge, an observer wrote: "It was the overflowing of pure sentiment, and united itself with the most tender sympathies of the heart. . . . Its spirit was that of a fond father, when he is committing his dearly beloved son to the government of himself. It was literally a lesson never to be forgotten."[3]

Although Emerson usually referred to Frost in his Journals as "the young preacher," the new minister was actually only a year younger than Emerson himself. He was born in Effingham, New Hampshire, on June 18, 1804. His father, a farmer, died when he was only two years old. Despite the handicap of poverty, he graduated from Harvard in 1830, and from the Divinity School in 1835, at the age of thirty-one. While at the Divinity School, he taught mathematics for a year to undergraduates. Following graduation, he preached at Northfield and at Barnstable prior to receiving a call to the Concord church.[4]

Frost at once began to make a place for himself in Concord. At town meeting in March, he was elected to the School Committee, as Emerson had been a year earlier.[5] In this position, he served faithfully and effectively for many years. There were three hundred families on his list for parish calls. And most of the burden of preaching fell on him also, for Dr. Ripley was almost ninety years of age and nearly blind.

For three months after the ordination, Emerson had no opportunity to sample the preaching of the new minister. He was supplying the pulpit in East Lexington both Sunday morning and afternoon; when absent from that pulpit, he was exchanging with other ministers. But in May, Emerson's old friend, Frederic Henry Hedge, agreed to take the East Lexington church for four Sundays, and Emerson was free to attend church in Concord.[6]

On May 7, Dr. Ripley baptized little Waldo, who wore the very same robe in which Emerson's brother Charles had once been christened. It was almost a year to the day since Charles's untimely death, and the parents could not help thinking of the "group of departed spirits . . . who hovered around the patriarch & the babe."[7] Barzillai Frost preached that day, and Emerson was not pleased. "I cannot hear the young men whose theological instruction is exclusively owed to Cambridge & to public institution," he wrote, "without feeling how much happier was my star which rained on me influences of ancestral religion." The Puritan tradition which had been handed down through a succession of ministers among his own forebears, and which he knew at first hand in his Aunt Mary, seemed to reveal a depth of religious sentiment which Barzillai Frost lacked. Education, thought Emerson, produces no more than "a normal piety . . . which only rarely devout genius could countervail."[8]

Emerson's dissatisfaction with Frost's preaching was so intense that he could not dismiss it from his mind. "I could ill dissemble my impatience at the show of instruction without one single real & penetrating word," he began once more.

> Here is a young man who has not yet learned the capital secret of his profession namely to convert life into truth. Not one single fact in all

his experience has he yet imported into his doctrine. & there he stands pitiable & magisterial, & without nausea reads page after page of mouth-filling words & seems to himself to be doing a deed. This man has ploughed & rode & talked & bought & sold he has read books, & eaten & drunk; his cow calves; his bull genders; he smiles & suffers & loves yet, all this experience is still aloof from his intellect; he has not converted one jot of it all into wisdom.

In all Frost's sermon, there was "not a surmise a hint . . . that he had ever lived at all. Not one line did he draw out of real history."[9] Two weeks later, when Emerson was stirred to renewed condemnation, he acknowledged that there was one thing that could be said for Frost's preaching: "Among provocatives, the next best thing to good preaching is bad preaching. I have even more thoughts during or enduring it than at other times."[10]

The dismal truth is that Barzillai Frost was a mediocre preacher. Emerson was not alone in thinking so; even Henry A. Miles frankly admitted as much, and he was Frost's most intimate friend. He had known Frost as a student in Cambridge, where they had been accustomed to go on walks together; and he had given the Right Hand of Fellowship at the ordination. "Doubtless you all early felt," he said at Frost's funeral, "that there was neither flexibility of voice, nor play of imagination, nor gush of emotion to give him, as a preacher, that power to which other endowments fairly entitled him." Frost's sermons were evidently delivered in a loud and positive monotone—a "ragged half screaming bass," as Emerson described it. So Miles tactfully acknowledged that "some did not sympathize fully with [Frost's] way of stating the case"; that "they felt that God had other methods also of commending his truth to human souls . . ."[11]

Among his colleagues in the Unitarian ministry, Frost was respected for the clarity of his mind at the same time that he was criticized for a certain narrowness in his perceptions. They always welcomed him at meetings of the local ministerial association, in the affairs of which he exerted great influence; for "if his opinions were not always accepted, if at times they seemed deficient in breadth, his lucid statement of them opened discussion, shed important cross-lights upon the subject, and brought out spirited replies from others, so that it came to be observed that his presence was enough to insure a good meeting of the Association."[12]

Frost's real abilities showed to better advantage throughout the week than on Sunday. "No small part of his sturdy influence was wielded in other places than the pulpit," Miles commented; "he was ready every-where for an earnest talk,—in the streets, in the fields; and few had more ability or relish for an improvised discussion." He was active in reform movements, especially temperance and antislavery. But above all, he was a devoted and successful parish minister: "one who through the week was diligent in your service, a guide of your schools, a coun-sellor at your firesides, a comforter at your sick and dying beds . . ." Throughout, he was blessed with "an unfailing cheerfulness and healthiness of mind"; so that for twenty years he went about Concord doing good, "daily lifting up this community to a higher tone . . ."[13]

Yet Frost's merits, and they were very genuine ones, were not of a sort to impress Emerson; while his liabilities were ones that Emerson would judge most harshly. Frost was a good shepherd of his flock; but Emerson, who had found pastoral duties uncongenial while minister of the Second Church, regarded them of secondary importance. Frost was civic-minded; but it required a very considerable provocation to rouse in Emerson a sense of community responsibility. What Emerson was looking for was a seer, a prophet, gifted with the power to transform the lives of men by the sheer magic of his eloquence. It is the end of eloquence, he declared, "in a half-hour's discourse,—perhaps by a few sentences,—to persuade a multitude of persons to renounce their opin-ions, and change the course of life."[14] This was the quality he looked for in the young preacher, and no other talents, however real, could compensate for its absence. It would be hard to conceive of anyone less fitted than Frost to satisfy Emerson at that particular juncture.

II

Emerson resumed his preaching at East Lexington on June 4, 1837, but he soon became so ill that he could do very little work. He went to Providence at the end of the week, as he had promised to do, to speak at the dedication of Hiram Fuller's school; but apart from that trip, he avoided all unnecessary exertion. He was suffering from an "inflammation on the lungs," and was doubtless fearful of consumption. He was still responsible for the preaching at East Lexington, but John Sullivan Dwight took his place for five Sundays, June 11 through July

9. He thought very seriously of taking a long trip for his health; but he ventured no farther than Plymouth, where Lidian, little Waldo, and he spent a week with her family. They were away on the Fourth of July, when the battle monument was dedicated at Concord and his hymn was sung. Barzillai Frost and Dr. Ripley both participated in the ceremonies. But by mid-July, Emerson's health had improved enough to permit him to resume preaching, and he was back in the pulpit at East Lexington on July 16. From that date until the end of November, he preached on all but three or four Sundays.[15]

On only one of Emerson's free Sundays is it clear that he went to hear Mr. Frost. On October 1, he noted in his Journal: "The young preacher preached from his ears & his memory, & never a word from his soul. His sermon was loud & hollow." But even on those Sundays when Emerson escaped the pain of listening to bad preaching, he did not avoid completely the man whose sermons distressed him. On October 15, on his return from Billerica, where he had preached all day, he had occasion to call on Frost at the latter's home. "I looked over the few books in the young clergyman's study yesterday till I shivered with cold Priestley; Noyes; Rosenmuller; Joseph Allen, & other Sunday School books; Schleusner; Norton; & the Saturday Night of Taylor; the dirty comfort of the farmer could easily seem preferable to the elegant poverty of the young clergyman."[16]

This catalogue of books and authors told Emerson, as it tells us, precisely what Frost's professional training had been and what his theological inclinations were. "The historical argument for Christianity, and that drawn from miracles," Henry Miles declared, "so completely convinced and satisfied [Frost's] mind, that he was never like a judge who gives a doubtful and timid decision, but rather like one who knows what he affirms, and therefore utters himself with confidence." Like his professors at the Divinity School, Frost believed that Christianity is a divinely inspired religion, attested by the miracles of Christ. The Bible is the only source of Christian truth, as distinguished from the truths of natural religion which may be determined by the use of the reason alone. Hence biblical criticism—Noyes, Rosenmüller, Schleusner, Norton—was regarded at Cambridge as the central core of ministerial training, for it made it possible for each student to determine for himself the truths of Christianity, uncorrupted by errors in the text and unperverted by human systems of doctrine. Time and time again Frost had reviewed the internal and external evidences of Christianity, especially the argument from miracles,

> . . . carefully examining one by one the multitude of points which they embrace, turning them over in a variety of lights, striking them all round to find if there was anywhere a flaw, or whether they would give the ring of sound metal; and the result had made him sure that here was a trustworthy reliance, here was solid ground, away from which everything to him was vague, shadowy, uncertain, and divested of authority.[17]

Emerson had been trained in these very same principles and had once accepted them, but by 1837, he had completely discarded them. In 1831, he could still preach—though not without uncertainty and fumbling—a sermon which restated the traditional doctrine of miracles. By 1833, he had discovered that the distinction between the Reason and the Understanding was "a philosophy itself." In January 1837, he made an extended application of this new philosophy in the lecture on religion which was one of the series he gave that winter in Boston. If every man possesses this transcendental Reason, if intuition of the absolute is possible for all, then the historical argument for a particular revelation attested by miracles shrivels into triviality.[18]

Into this realm of vague speculation, as he regarded it, Frost had no desire to venture. "Through life he concerned himself with those thoughts which he could apprehend with clearness and certainty," Henry Miles recorded. "He knew exactly the point where any subject shaded off into poetry, or sentiment, or mysticism, and at that point he dropped it."[19] Emerson could not help but feel that Frost was imprisoned in an immature phase of belief that he had himself outgrown. Part of the extraordinary vehemence of his reaction to Frost's theology may well have stemmed from the fact that he was condemning a part of his earlier self. In religion it sometimes happens that the intensest reaction occurs when the convert is confronted by those whom he has left behind.

III

In December 1837 and January 1838, Emerson was busy preparing and delivering a series of lectures in Boston on "Human Culture." Evidently he wanted to clear his schedule of competing obligations; for, on

November 16, he wrote to William Silsbee, asking him to take the East Lexington pulpit for eight to ten Sabbaths, beginning the first Sunday in December. His concentration on his lectures seems to have kept him home on Sundays, for there is only one reference to preaching in that period in the Journals. On December 3, Emerson's half-uncle, Samuel Ripley, preached in Concord. Curiously enough, this was the day when Mrs. Emerson remarked that "it is wicked to go to church Sundays." Emerson's reaction was more favorable. "Sunday I could not help remarking at church how much humanity was in the preaching of my good uncle, Mr R. The rough farmers had their hands at their eyes repeatedly. But the old hardened sinners, the arid educated men, ministers & others, were dry as stones."[20]

In February 1838, the lectures at last over, there remained "a harvest of small works to be done which were adjourned to this day." But there was also a major decision to be reached. For something like two years, Emerson had served as stated supply at East Lexington. On February 18, he told the committee there that he wished to put off his charge, and he recommended John Sullivan Dwight as his successor. The committee assented, even though the term of his engagement still had time left to run, provided he would take on himself the responsibility for securing Dwight's services.[21]

Emerson's decision was more than a farewell to East Lexington; it was actually the cutting of the last thread that bound him "to that prized gown & band the symbols black & white of old & distant Judah." This decision had been a long time in the making. Ever since graduation from Harvard in 1821, he had been involved in a quest for an appropriate calling. The ministry had originally attracted him because of his "passionate love for the strains of eloquence." He thought of the sermon as an appropriate vehicle for the inspired utterance of which he regarded himself capable: "The office of a clergyman is twofold; public preaching & private influence. Entire success in the first is the lot of few, but this I am encouraged to expect." When he relinquished the charge of the Second Church in 1832, he was prompted by complex and partly obscure motives; but involved in the decision was undoubtedly his distaste for pastoral duties. After his return from Europe, he welcomed opportunities for occasional preaching, since he could pursue the part of the calling of the minister that appealed to him and avoid the pastoral duties which were uncongenial.[22]

Preaching was a more restrictive mode of utterance than lecturing, however, and it was doubtless with relief that he found that his growing reputation as a lecturer would permit him to abandon the pulpit altogether. To his mother he wrote: "But henceforth perhaps I shall live by lecturing which promises to be good bread. I have relinquished my ecclesiastical charge at E Lexington & shall not preach more except from the Lyceum." The lecture platform offered all the advantages of the pulpit in heightened degree, with none of the disadvantages: "Here he may lay himself out utterly, large, enormous, prodigal, on the subject of the hour. Here he may dare to hope for ecstasy & eloquence."[23]

Emerson's last Sunday at East Lexington was March 25. While he preached on three other occasions in 1838, at New York, Waltham, and Watertown, his departure from East Lexington was really the end of his career as a minister. As a kind of gesture of defiance, on March 25 and the later occasions when he did preach, a large part of the sermon was made up of extracts from the Boston lecture on religion, so that his pulpit utterances at the end became more explicitly and uncompromisingly transcendental than they had ever been before.[24]

The final break with the calling to which he had been consecrated was not an easy one. That he was distinctly upset by the decision, even though he was confident it was the right one, is apparent from the Journals. It seems to be no mere coincidence that it was in March 1838, after he had sought release from East Lexington and before his final appearance in the pulpit there, that his castigation of the churches and of Frost's preaching became most severe. At such a time, he was not a reporter, objectively appraising the state of organized religion. He was a man arguing with himself, trying to be reassured that the blame for his action lay not within him, but with society. For his own peace of mind, he had to persuade himself that it was the world that had failed, and not Ralph Waldo Emerson.

On Sunday, March 4, he warned: "Let the clergy beware when the well disposed scholar begins to say, 'I cannot go to church, time is too precious.' " On Sunday, March 18, a stormy, snowy day, the very length of the Journal entry is a clue to the emotional turmoil which he concealed beneath a serene exterior:

> At Church all day but almost tempted to say I would go no more. Men go where they are wont to go else had no soul gone this afternoon. The snowstorm was real the preacher merely spectral. Vast contrast to look

at him & then out of the window. Yet no fault in the good man.
Evidently he thought himself a faithful searching preacher, mentioned
that he thought so several times; & seemed to be one of that large
class, *sincere persons based on shams; sincere persons who are bred
& do live in shams.* He had lived in vain. He had no one word inti-
mating that ever he had laughed or wept, was married or enamoured,
had been cheated, or voted for, or chagrined. If he had ever lived &
acted we were none the wiser for it. It seemed strange they should
come to Church. It seemed as if their own houses were very unenter-
taining that they should prefer this thoughtless clamorous young
person. . . .

There is no better subject for effective writing than the Clergy. I
ought to sit & think & then write a discourse to the American clergy
showing them the ugliness & unprofitableness of theology & churches
at this day & the glory & sweetness of the moral nature out of whose
pale they are almost wholly shut. . . .

The men I have spoke of above—sincere persons who live in shams,
are those who accept another man's consciousness for their own, & are
in the state of a son who should always suck at his mothers teat. I
think Swedenborg ought so to represent them or still more properly,
as permanent embryos which received all their nourishment through
the umbilical cord & never arrived at a conscious & independent existence.

Once leave your own knowledge of God, your own sentiment, &
take a secondary knowledge, as St Paul's, or George Fox's, or Swedenborg's, and you get wider from God with every year this secondary
form lasts; & if, as now, eighteen centuries; why, the chasm yawns to
that breadth that men can scarcely be convinced there is in them anything divine.[25]

No doubt, through all this period of Emerson's inner struggle,
Barzillai Frost was wholly ignorant of what was going on. He was of
course not one to whom Emerson would turn directly for spiritual
comfort. Yet in a curious inverted way, and quite unaware of the fact,
Frost was in a position to give Emerson precisely what he wanted.
Emerson had to believe that the institutions of religion and the calling
of the ministry, to which he had once been dedicated, no longer de-
served his support. Frost's deficiencies as a preacher made it easy for
Emerson to persuade himself that the churches generally were in decay.
One wonders, however, how he would have solved his problem had the
pulpit in Concord been occupied by a minister more conspicuously
gifted in pulpit utterance. One wonders what kind of a Divinity

School Address there would have been had Barzillai Frost possessed some of the eloquence of his beloved teacher, Henry Ware, Jr.

IV

By a strange quirk of fate, it was just at this juncture that Emerson received a letter from a committee of the senior class of the Divinity School in Cambridge. They desired him to deliver before them, the following July, "the customary discourse, on occasion of their entering upon the active Christian ministry." They thought of him as still a clergyman, and so addressed him as "Rev. R. W. Emerson." Curiously enough, in his reply to them, he did not reject that identification with the calling of the ministry, but rather explicitly accepted it: "In the good hope of our calling," he wrote, "I am your friend and servant . . ."[26]

Emerson might well have regarded this invitation as providential, offering as it did an outlet for all the festering irritations that had thus far been confined to the Journals. But July 15 was almost four months away, and even before that date arrived, his mood had begun to change. He continued to condemn bad preaching—though not always Frost's preaching—and he continued to comment on the decaying state of religion and the churches. The note of personal involvement diminished, however. A nagging doubt appeared: if the church is dead, why is it that so many good people seem unaware of the fact? The stormy, snowy Sunday of March 18, then, was the final climax of Emerson's crisis of vocation. July 15, seen in the context of this problem, brought public proclamation in disguised form of his conviction that he did not belong in the ministry, because that calling did not allow scope for his special talents and ambitions.

Meanwhile, there were more Sundays at church, and new occasions to consider the great themes of religion. On Sunday, April 1, Emerson was in Cambridge, discussing Theism with some of the theological students. He had been doubtful about the venture, but it turned out far better than he had expected. Later that week, he went to New York, where he preached, on April 8, two of his transcendentalized sermons in Orville Dewey's church. On April 22, he was at a teachers' meeting of the Sunday School, which Frost very likely attended also, at which the question of miracles was broached. Emerson's position was, of course, that Jesus needs no miracles to attest his divine origin. "Well then he must have credentials & miracle is the Credentials. I answer God sends me messengers alway. I am surrounded by messengers of God who show me credentials day by day."[27]

On Friday, May 18, Emerson evidently encountered Frost making the rounds of his parish. Emerson himself had never enjoyed the routine of parish calling, and he felt no special need of a visit in the traditional manner from the local minister. So far as he could see, Frost was simply imitating men like Dr. Charles Lowell and Henry Ware, Jr., who had won for themselves extraordinary reputations as parish ministers. He thereby doomed himself to mediocrity:

> The young preacher comes to his parish & learns there are 300 families which he must visit each once in a year. In stead of groping to get exactly the old threads of relation to bind him to the people that bound his venerable predecessor, let him quit all leather & twine let him so highly & gladly entertain his most poetic & exhilerating office as to cast all this nonsense of false expectation & drivelling Chinese secondariness behind him, & acquaint them at first hand with Deity.[28]

The real duty of the minister, Emerson insisted, is prophetic utterance, not parish calling:

> Let him not be anxious to get out to see in civil sort his 300 families with tablebook to know the times how oft & when. Perhaps it is mere folly for him to visit one. But let him when he meets one of these men or women be to them divine man be to them thought & virtue let their timid aspirations find in him a friend let their trampled instincts be genially tempted out in the mellow atmosphere of his society, let their doubts know that he hath doubted and their wonder feel that he has wondered. . . . Discharge to them the priestly office, & absent or present you shall be followed with their veneration & grappled to them by love.[29]

The entry for Sunday, May 27, presents a problem in identification.[30] "Nettled again & nervous (as much as sometimes by flatulency or piddling things)," Emerson wrote, "by the wretched Sundays preaching of Mr H." Evidently Frost was not the only preacher who rubbed him the wrong way. Of the Cambridge men with the appropriate initial, the most plausible candidate would be Frederic Henry Hedge, who

was down from Bangor on a visit at about that time, as was his custom
every year in May. Whoever it was, he "droned & droned & wound his
stertorous horn upon the main doctrine of Xty the resurrection, namely,
& how little it was remembered in modern preaching, & modern prayers . . ."[31]

Late in May, Dr. Ripley suffered an ill turn, but he recovered enough
to preach on Sunday, June 17. Emerson ordinarily respected the vener-
able minister, even though he tended to look upon him as a quaint survival of a bygone age. On occasion, he had contrasted him favorably
with the Biblical critics from Cambridge: "Homely & dry his things are
because they are traditions accepted for nature. . . . But you do not
feel cheated & empty as when fed by the grammarians." This time,
however, Emerson ridiculed the way in which, at the morning service,
Ripley identified the sick and bereaved in his prayers by enumerating
"all the degrees of kin selecting & specifying each with botanical precision." In the afternoon, the comment on the half-blind preacher, then
in his eighty-eighth year, was even less charitable: "This afternoon, the
foolishest preaching—which bayed at the moon. Go, hush, old man,
whom years have taught no truth. . . . Such Moabitish darkness, well
typified in the perplexity about his glasses, reminded one of the squash-
bugs who stupid stare at you when you lift the rotten leaf of the
vines."[32]

On Sunday, June 24, the Journal entry is far mellower at the beginning than at the end, as though the morning service had been more
satisfactory than the afternoon one. There is no clue, however, to the
identity of the preacher or preachers. In the morning, Emerson even
discerned "poetry concealed in all the commonplaces of prayer 'Searcher
of Hearts' &c"; and he described the "softness & peace, the benignant
humanity that hovers over our assembly when it sits down in the morning service in Church. . . ." By afternoon, the familiar contrast between traditional religion and spontaneous faith had reasserted itself
with its usual vigor:

> The faith should blend with the light of rising & of setting suns, with
> the flying cloud, the blooming clover, & the breath of flowers; But now
> the Sabbath, the priest's Sabbath has long lost the splendor of nature,
> it is unlovely, we are glad when it is done, we can make, we do make,
> even in the presence of his, a far better, holier, sweeter, for ourselves.[33]

V

On July 1, Emerson was once again in his pew both morning and afternoon, but got little enough from the experience. Preachers should be informed, he felt, that Sunday is the only time some of their parishioners have for thought; and so "do not defraud them of that, as miserably as two men have me today."[34] By this time, the appointed day for the address to the students in Cambridge was only a fortnight away; and Emerson, hard at work on his manuscript, was intolerant of distractions. Even the Journal tended to be neglected, and the frequency and length of the entries dropped off as he applied himself to the task at hand.

The first part of the Divinity School Address seems to have been freshly composed for the occasion. To be sure, it follows a pattern of ideas that Emerson had used before. The sermon on "Summer," composed in 1829 and preached as recently as 1837, also begins with a poetic description of nature which leads to the discovery of God (or a divine mind) which is the underlying and everpresent reality.[35] But none of the actual phrasing of the Address was taken from that sermon, nor did Emerson borrow from the transcendental lecture on religion that he had been using recently whenever he was asked to preach.

As soon as Emerson began to discuss "the famine of our churches," however, he turned to his Journals. For over a year, he had been complaining to himself about Barzillai Frost, who preached so badly and thought parish calling so important. These passages needed almost no alteration to serve his purpose. Some of the changes he made were stylistic. Where once he had written: "the flying cloud, the blooming clover, & the breath of flowers," he now substituted: "the flying cloud, the singing bird, and the breath of flowers"; for he had already used "the blowing clover" in another passage. Some of the alterations were in the interest of propriety; this address was hardly the occasion to refer to the local clergy as "permanent embryos," still receiving nourishment through the umbilical cord. Other deletions were made to avoid specific mention of particular individuals, like Dr. Lowell and the younger Henry Ware.[36]

Such emendations were not made simply to avoid embarrassment to local worthies. Emerson's avowed purpose was to "convert life into truth," to perceive the general truth in the particular event. His method was commonly the substitution of generalized expressions for specific names and episodes. The result is often no more than a stylistic device, in which the general statement is a transparent cloak for the event that occasioned it. The alert reader then has little difficulty in converting truth back into life, into the biography of the author.

Hence the Divinity School Address may be read on two levels. Its manifest content is the enduring message that the life of religion must be re-created anew in the souls of each successive generation of men. Its hidden meaning is an apology for casting aside the prized gown and band, and an assertion that society—symbolized here by Barzillai Frost—was responsible for the outcome. Almost every word of the crucial paragraph beginning: "Whenever the pulpit is usurped by a formalist," was inspired by Frost, and most of it can be traced to March 18, 1838, when Emerson's inner turmoil over his crisis of vocation was the greatest.

Evidently, Emerson's generalizations represent less reliable evidence than has usually been supposed as to the condition of religion and the churches at that day. No one would ever guess, from reading his comments, that the Divinity School in Cambridge in the 1830s was an institution of extraordinary vitality; that it was exploring new fields of Biblical scholarship; that it was alive to all sorts of social issues; that some of the most promising young men of the region were enrolled as students; and that a very high proportion of them went on to distinguished careers in a variety of professions, including the parish ministry.[37] Emerson's oft-quoted phrase, "the pale negations of Boston Unitarianism," tells us a good deal about his standard of values, but it is hardly the final word on the religion of William Ellery Channing, Henry Ware, Jr., or even Andrews Norton.

Despite Emerson's ruthless criticisms of Frost, he bore him no personal ill will or animosity. Emerson had come to regard Frost as representative of the clergy of the day; in criticizing him, the intent was to condemn the type of which he served as symbol. Yet the fact remains that Emerson's judgment of the clergy at large was deeply colored by his experience of the one man who was generally recognized as unsuccessful in the pulpit.

Emerson himself must have realized that the opinion of a man in his position might be clouded by personal interest, for he made a con-

scious attempt to avoid bias. But by July 8, he felt that he had passed
beyond any personal involvement in the problem he was discussing:

> But when I have as clear a sense as now that I am speaking simple
> truth without any bias, any foreign interest in the matter,—all rail-
> ing, all unwillingness to hear, all danger of injury to the conscience,
> dwindles & disappears. I refer to the discourse now growing under my
> eye to the Divinity School.

His mission, he told himself, would be legitimate only if he were able
to achieve an attitude of entire detachment: "In preparing to go to
Cambridge with my speech to the young men . . . it occurred with
force that I had no right to go unless I were equally willing to be prevented from going."[38]

VI

Where was Barzillai Frost on the evening of July 15? For the sake of
dramatic fitness, he should have been in the little chapel of Divinity
Hall in Cambridge, but there is no evidence that he was there and the
probabilities are strong that he was not. We have testimony as to the
presence of Henry Ware, Jr. and Dean Palfrey, of Elizabeth Peabody,
Theodore Parker, and Cyrus Bartol. But regarding the minister from
Concord, the record is silent.

For two weeks, while Emerson was completing the manuscript of his
address, Frost had been occupied with a chore that has heretofore been
his sole claim to remembrance. On June 25, 1838, the "immediate government" of Harvard College took note of the case of a member of the
senior class who had been all too frequently absent from both prayers
and recitations. The culprit was James Russell Lowell, a son of the
Reverend Charles Lowell, whose classmates had just elected him class
poet. The action of the faculty was precipitated by an unfortunate inci-
dent at evening prayers when Lowell, who had spent the day celebrat-
ing his election, arose in his seat and bowed ceremoniously and low to
the congregation, first on his right hand and then on his left. The
faculty voted "that Lowell, senior, . . . be suspended till the Saturday
before Commencement, to pursue his studies with Mr. Frost of Concord, to recite to him twice a day, reviewing the whole of Locke's
'Essay' and studying also Mackintosh's 'Review of Ethical Philosophy,'

to be examined in both on his return, and not to visit Cambridge during the period of his suspension."[39]

Young Lowell did not relish his rustication "up here at this infernal Concord," but the experience was not a total loss. He enjoyed long walks, sometimes alone in the moonlight, sometimes to the cliffs with Mr. Emerson. He attended sociables, flirted with Caroline Brooks, and wrote sentimental verses in praise of her black eyes, pretty smile, and gentle heart. She ran in his head and heart, he acknowledged, "more than she has any right to"; but it was well understood that Rockwood Hoar had the inside track, so Lowell stood aside.[40]

Though Lowell was forbidden to go to Cambridge to see his friends, there was nothing to prevent them from visiting him in exile. The Frosts were unfailingly hospitable, and put them up overnight. "Our ride from C. was exceedingly pleasant, after the shower and Mr F's hospitality," Nathan Hale wrote to his classmate. The one thing he did find to criticize about "the *permaxime* hospitable Bar" was that "his *bed is too soft* for this *hot weather.*" He proposed to arrange for Frost to preach at Andover on exchange, "and give him a taste of the delights of feathers, and ther. 90° in the shade—."[41]

The Frosts had been married for just over a year, and Mrs. Frost had the care of a two-months-old baby; but she still found time to think of Lowell's comfort. "I hope you will find your hostess a 'good sort of woman' and a fine housekeeper as I hear she is," Hale had written, "to say nothing of finding her a pleasant and intelligent lady." Lowell readily assented. "Mrs. Frost is simply the best woman I ever set my eyes on," he wrote back. "Always pleasant, always striving to make me happy and comfortable, and always with a sweet smile, a very sweet smile! She *is* a jewel! Then, too, I love her all the better for that she loves that husband of hers, and she does love him and cherish him." He would marry her "as a reward for so much virtue," were she not already married, and old enough to be his mother, or at any rate, his eldest sister. "That woman has really reconciled me to Concord."[42]

With Frost himself, Lowell got on at least amicably. "I shall do my best to please Mr. F.," he wrote soon after his arrival, "since I find he does his best to please me & make me comfortable." As time went on, however, he found out how best to exploit his tutor's weaknesses. Though an admirer of Locke, Frost did not hesitate on occasion to take exception to minor parts of the Lockean philosophy. Lowell would stoutly defend the philosopher and needle Frost into an extended digression which would take up three quarters of the allotted time. "The man's cardinal fault is that he delights to hear the sound of his own voice," Lowell complained. Sooner or later, Frost would stumble into a particularly flimsy argument, whereupon Lowell would burst out "with greater fury for having been pent up so long, like a simmering volcano."[43]

On Sundays, Lowell went to church. One day, his tutor referred in the sermon to Niagara Falls, " 'Where,' he said, 'a vast body of water nearly *half a mile wide* & *several feet deep,* urged on by the superincumbent weight of lakes, plunges as it were into the middle of the Earth.' ! ! ! ! ! That's literal." This excerpt may well represent Barzillai Frost's preaching at its worst, but there is no escape from the universal testimony: pulpit utterance was not his great gift.[44]

VII

The storm of reproach that burst over Emerson following his address came as a surprise to him. He met the attacks with outward serenity and refused to be drawn into controversy; yet, as Stephen Whicher has pointed out, inwardly he was decidedly upset. He received a sudden reminder that the world of fact might not yield to his assertion of the ideal; that however eloquently he might proclaim the mountains to be moving, they still stood fast. "The reception of the *Address*," Professor Whicher has said, "was an angular intrusion of fact into the smooth world of his thoughts, which, while rousing him to an unprecedented vigor of defiance, helped to undermine in the long run his capacity to identify the ideal and the real."[45]

If the Address thus proved crucial in the inward and cosmic drama of Emerson's ideas, it also was a turning point in the outward and parochial matter of his relationship with Barzillai Frost. While Emerson's antipathy to Frost from mid-1837 to mid-1838 was directed at Frost the symbol rather than at Frost the man, it was nonetheless real. But once Emerson had solved the problem of his relationship to the profession of which Frost was the symbol, he was able to confront Frost the man with composure. It was no longer necessary for him to suffer through Frost's sermons in order to reassure himself that the church was tottering to its fall, so he worshipped instead in the woods and fields. He could then meet Frost in other relationships without being aroused to condemnation, so that their contacts, though never intimate, were wholly friendly.

In the months following the address, Emerson attended church less and less often. He had previously gone regularly, except when he was off preaching himself, or when he was preparing lectures under pressure. The evidence in the Journals is admittedly meagre, but it is fairly clear that by the fall of 1839 he had given up Sunday churchgoing almost entirely. Furthermore, between July 1838 and September 1839, while he sometimes commented on bad preaching, he did so less often, more briefly, and with far less emotional intensity than he had previously been wont to do.

Emerson was in church on Sunday, August 19, 1838, when Dr. Ripley preached, and again a week later. On September 16, he had a good word for poor Barzillai Frost: "Mr Frost said very happily in today's sermon, 'We see God in nature as we see the soul of our friend in his countenance.' " On January 6, 1839, he was present when Communion was celebrated. On March 3, the singing pleased him; but on March 10, when he went to both morning and afternoon services, he charged the church "with a want of respect to the soul of the worshipper." He liked the silent church before the service, he said, better than any preaching. On April 7, he heard the sermon that he afterwards condemned in the essay on "Compensation"; but the record does not show whether Frost was the guilty preacher. On May 12, he commented: "All or almost all that I hear at Church is mythological." On the following Sunday, he repeated the charge that the preacher was not dealing with real life: "Cease, O thou unauthorized talker, to prate of consolation, & resignation, and spiritual joys, in neat & balanced sentences."[46]

The last clear reference in the Journals to churchgoing at Concord occurs in September 1839. "I love the Sunday morning," he wrote on Saturday, September 28. "I hail it from afar. I wake with gladness & a holiday feeling always on that day. The Church is ever my desk. If I did not go thither I should not write so many of these wayward pages." The next day found him in church, where he praised the singing and criticized Frost—"O thou hoarse preacher"—for exhorting, and preaching cant. In the months that followed, he may have gone to church a few times, for there are one or two ambiguous entries in the Journals, but his churchgoing was essentially a thing of the past. When pleasant weather came in the spring of 1840, a suggestion of Sunday morning walks appears: "We can never see Christianity from Christendom but from the pastures, from a boat in the pond, from the song of a starling, we possibly may."[47]

Other members of the Emerson family continued to go to church, and Emerson never discouraged them from going. "He was glad to have us go to church," his son recalled. "His own attitude in the matter was, that it was only a question for each person where the best church was,—in the solitary wood, the chamber, the talk with the serious friend, or in hearing the preacher." He did not actually resign his membership in the First Parish until 1852, and he continued after that date to pay the equivalent of his parish tax as a voluntary contribution.[48]

While Frost never became intimate with his parishioner, the two men were on friendly terms. In June 1839, Frost was the spokesman for a group of Concord citizens who made a present of books to Emerson "as a slight expression of the worth of your lectures to themselves & families." In 1841, Emerson sent Frost a copy of the Essays, which Frost acknowledged in a letter written in the mannered and formal style of the day. In 1842, it was Emerson who took Frost to call on Hawthorne; but Hawthorne had even less respect for the clergy than Emerson. "He is a good sort of hum-drum parson enough," he recorded in his Notebooks, "and well fitted to increase the stock of manuscript sermons, of which there must be a fearful quantity already in the world." In 1847, Frost received a copy of Emerson's poems, which struck him as a higher expression of the author's mind than anything he had previously published. For several years, too, Emerson and Frost were two of the three curators of the Concord Lyceum, and jointly made arrangements for the winter schedule of speakers.[49]

Frost served as minister in Concord for twenty years. Apart from the preaching, his ministry there was successful, though not entirely free from disagreements within the parish. He was still in his early fifties, however, when his health began to fail, and he was obliged to seek a warmer climate during the coldest months of the year. He spent several weeks at St. Thomas and Santa Cruz in February and March 1856, and returned there the following winter. It became apparent in the fall of 1857 that his recovery was very doubtful, and so he resigned his pastorate on October 3. The winter of 1857–58, spent at Fayal in the Azores, proved to be a tragic one. The state of his health continually worsened; but even that shadow was obliterated by the accidental death of his younger son, aged ten, who fell from a cliff and died after more than two days of intense suffering. (Two daughters had previously died in infancy.) The Frosts returned to Concord, where death came on December 8, 1858.[50]

In his twilight years, Emerson once more began to attend church on Sundays. By that time, Grindall Reynolds had been minister for a dozen years or more, and the image of Barzillai Frost was fast fading away.[51]

THE MINISTER AS REFORMER:

Profiles of Unitarian Ministers in the Antislavery Reform

Two generations ago George Willis Cooke assessed the record of the Unitarians in respect to antislavery in these terms: "In proportion to its numbers no religious body in the country did so much to promote the antislavery reform as the Unitarian." No Unitarian minister defended slavery from the pulpit, he declared, although many did not approve of the methods or extreme measures of the abolitionists. "The desire of Unitarians to be just, rational, and open-minded, exposed many of them to the criticism of being neither for nor against slavery. But it is certain that they were not indifferent to its evils nor recreant to their humanitarian principles."[1]

This appraisal is rather more favorable than many commentators have thought justified. The Reverend Samuel J. May, himself a Garrisonian abolitionist, acknowledged that many individual Unitarians had performed honorable service in the cause of antislavery; but the record of the denomination, as such, he characterized as a "discreditable account" of "proslavery conduct." The Unitarians in their corporate actions, he insisted, were anything but impartial, courageous, or Christian in their dealings with the issue. "But let the sad truth be plainly told," he wrote in 1868, "as a solemn warning to all coming generations, that even the Unitarians, as a body, were corrupted and morally paralyzed by our national consenting with slaveholders . . ."[2] John Haynes Holmes concurred with May when he declared, in 1908, that the Unitarian church was as guilty as any other of "base desertion of the one cause in the nineteenth century that was unmistakably the cause of God."[3]

Sweeping judgments of this sort may have some homiletical usefulness, but they are of questionable value to the historian. Nor does it help matters to take refuge in the happy thought that the truth doubt-less lies somewhere between the two extremes. What is needed, instead, is an analysis of the variety and range of Unitarian attitudes towards antislavery, together with some attempt to assess the various factors involved in the shaping of opinion. The cleavage between abolitionist and gradualist is easy to discern. The former called for the immediate end of slavery, and insisted that a resolute refusal to compromise with evil and with the institutions that supported it would doom it. The latter argued that long-standing evils can never be quickly eradicated; they sought to contain the Slave Power, as they termed it, in order to mobilize legal and moral pressure for its ultimate defeat.

But it is not enough simply to categorize Unitarians in terms of the solutions they proposed and the methods they advocated. It is essential to note the interplay of other factors, such as these: (a) the differences among Unitarians with respect to the time or occasion when they be-came deeply interested in, rather than casually aware of, the issue of slavery; (b) the extent to which they made the antislavery issue cen-tral in their concerns; (c) the differences that evidently existed in a number of churches between ministers and laity; and (d) the varying opinions held with respect to the proper role in social action to be played by organized religious bodies, as distinguished from the re-ligiously motivated activity of individuals. A full-scale study of the Uni-tarian involvement in the antislavery reform, conceived on a scale ample enough to take into consideration such factors, is much to be desired. Meanwhile, the interplay among them may be suggested by a sketch of three ministers, representing three different positions held by Uni-tarians on this issue.

I

Before the war, there were only a handful of Unitarian churches in the slave states. The *Unitarian Register* for 1850 lists nine, but the pulpits of two of them were vacant. The secretary of the American Unitarian Association, on more than one occasion, had found it diffi-cult to persuade men to candidate or even to supply pulpits in the South, and the experience of such men as did venture into the slave states was, to say the least, often an unhappy one.[4] Some men, like Samuel Gilman of Charleston, South Carolina, seem to have survived by saying nothing directly about slavery. Yet only one minister, Theodore Clapp of New Orleans, was known as an apologist for it.[5] Not even the Garrisonians, who scrutinized all ministers with an inquisitorial eye, were able to find others in that category, however much they might complain that the failure of various moderates to come out strongly on the side of human freedom lent aid and comfort to the proslavery cause.[6]

Setting Clapp aside as a special case, at least three general categories of Unitarian ministers may be distinguished. There were, first of all, the abolitionists, who called for the immediate end of slavery without compensation to the slaveholders. The Unitarian abolitionists may be further discriminated into subcategories. Some, like Samuel J. May and his cousin Samuel May, Jr., were closely associated with Garrison and active in the affairs of the antislavery societies. Others, like Theodore Parker and Thomas Wentworth Higginson, went to school to the Garrisonians, but did not accept their rather doctrinaire position on political action and nonresistance. Finally, a number of men, like James Freeman Clarke and William H. Furness, were never officers or managers of the antislavery societies, but were willing to speak at their public meetings and be more or less identified with the abolitionists in the public mind.[7] It should be noted that none of the Unitarian abolitionists were so-called "new organization" men. That is to say, in the divisions in the abolitionist ranks that took place in 1839 and 1840 over the issues of women's rights and political action, the Unitarians stayed with Garrison. It does not appear that any of them left the Massachusetts Anti-Slavery Society to join the rival Massachusetts Abolition Society, or the American Anti-Slavery Society to join the rival American and Foreign Anti-Slavery Society.

Most Unitarian ministers, though antislavery, were not abolitionists and took pains to dissociate themselves from the Garrisonians. They were gradualists, who in due course became free-soilers, insisting on the containment of slavery within its traditional boundaries, and relying on the development of a more enlightened public opinion to support public policy that would bring about its eventual extinction. It is hard to find a plausible way to distinguish subcategories of this large group, unless it be by noting that their antislavery sentiments were increasingly fed by the political encroachments of the Slave Power, so that different members of the group were stirred to action at different times by successive political crises. The conscience of William Ellery Channing might be pricked by the example of the abolitionists in the 1830s, but Henry W. Bellows was not much aroused until the Mexican War. And there were ·others who did not reach the same degree of involvement until the passage of the Fugitive Slave Law, or even the rendition of Anthony Burns in 1854. These men had, if you will, somewhat different boiling points; and it took twenty years from the time of the publication of Channing's book on *Slavery* (1835) for the boiling process to be substantially completed.

One additional group must be noted separately, however, if only because its members were repeatedly singled out for bitter condemnation by the abolitionists. Among them were the ministers of some of the most prominent and influential churches in Boston and elsewhere, such as Francis Parkman of the New North Church, Ezra Stiles Gannett of Federal Street, and Orville Dewey of the Church of the Messiah in New York. While the argument that religious bodies as such should not take a stand on political issues was not peculiar to them, they found it especially congenial. It seems to be significant that many of these men had joined the American Colonization Society at an early date. Unlike a good many other colonizationists, however, they did not advance to more radical ground when the colonization movement came under abolitionist attack in the 1830s.[8] Yet they were not officers of the Colonization Society, or prominent at its meetings, and so were not identified conspicuously in the public mind with that group. The abolitionists did not attack them as colonizationists, but simply as moderates whose extreme caution was playing into the hands of the Slave Power.

II

Of the Unitarian abolitionists, none is a more appealing figure than Samuel J. May, minister successively at Brooklyn, Connecticut; South Scituate, Massachusetts; and Syracuse, New York. Outspoken in his condemnation of slavery, he never became abusive in his criticism, nor did he question the integrity or motives of those with whom he disagreed. Although firm in his support of Garrison and the antislavery societies, he never became one of those fanatics who insist that the world must rotate around their own chosen reform. Despite the fact that he was early identified with a hated and despised group, he himself nevertheless seems to have made no enemies.

May dated his antislavery views from the year 1821, when he saw manicled slaves while on a trip to Baltimore, Washington, and Richmond.[9] It was not until 1830, however, that he was drawn actively into the abolitionist ranks. In October of that year, while on a visit to Boston, he went with Bronson Alcott, his brother-in-law, and Samuel E. Sewall, a cousin, to one of the meetings arranged by Garrison in the Julien Hall. Deeply impressed by Garrison's condemnation of the colonization scheme, with which he had previously been sympathetic, and by Garrison's insistence on immediate, unconditional emancipation, May and his two companions introduced themselves, offered their support, and invited Garrison to Alcott's lodgings, where they all talked until midnight. "That night," May afterwards testified, "my soul was baptized in his spirit, and ever since I have been a disciple and fellow-laborer of William Lloyd Garrison."[10]

May was soon drawn into various abolitionist activities. In May, 1831, he delivered a sermon on slavery at Ralph Waldo Emerson's church, which was duly advertised and reported in the *Liberator*.[11] When the New England (afterwards the Massachusetts) Anti-Slavery Society was organized in 1832, he became one of the vice presidents; and he was active at the Philadelphia convention in 1833 which promulgated a Declaration of Sentiments of the Garrisonians.[12] He was elected a vice president of the American Anti-Slavery Society for which the Philadelphia convention prepared the way, and served almost every year thereafter either as vice president or manager. Meanwhile, in 1833, he had been drawn in as a close adviser and supporter of Prudence Crandall, whose attempt to carry on a school for "Young Ladies and Little Misses of color" in Canterbury, Connecticut, adjacent to Brooklyn, was brutally broken up by the townspeople.[13] For fourteen months, in 1835 and 1836, he served as General Agent of the Massachusetts Anti-Slavery Society, a post later filled by his cousin, Samuel May, Jr. In short, in the 1830s especially and to a somewhat diminished extent thereafter, May was deeply involved in the organizational activities of the abolitionist societies.

May always spoke with respect and affection of Garrison, yet it is clear that he tried to be a moderating influence on the more intemperate abolitionists. "I respect and love Garrison's fervent devotion to the cause of the oppressed," May wrote, "and his fearlessness in reproving the oppressors; but no one can disapprove, more than I do, the harshness of his epithets, and the bitterness of his invectives."[14] He pleaded with Theodore Parker and Horace Mann not to resort to sarcasm; even the invectives of Jesus, his son recalled, gave him disquiet.[15] Entirely characteristic of him was his behavior on one occasion in 1844, when he attempted to tone down the harsh language of a resolution presented by Garrison at a meeting of the Massachusetts Anti-Slavery Society. Garrison had declared of the American Church "which perpetrates all these enormous crimes" that it "is not the Church of Christ, but the synagogue of Satan." May tried, quite without success, to substitute the word "permits" for "perpetrates," and to eliminate altogether the last five words.[16]

May was also much more ready than Garrison to acknowledge some good in the nonabolitionist antislavery men. When John Quincy Adams aroused the ire of the true believers by announcing that he would not vote for the abolition of slavery in the District of Columbia until local sentiment supported such a measure, it was May who reminded his associates of the great service Adams had rendered to the cause. "It would be most unjust, ungrateful, and unwise, in abolitionists," he warned, "to withdraw their confidence from Mr. Adams."[17] In meetings of reformers, his plea was repeatedly for the inclusion of men of good will, even though not all of them agreed with a strict party line. Though he was criticized for so doing by Parker Pillsbury and Garrison, he invited Gerrit Smith and other advocates of political action to a convention at Syracuse in 1850.[18] As he put it on an earlier occasion:

> If my brother differs from me in this Society, I have, I ought to have, no wish to turn him out, or to make him feel uncomfortable in remaining in association with me. I want to change his heart—nothing else. . . . When this wish to force assent or to punish the honest expression of opinions has obtained possession of a man's mind, he loses all his moral power,—he ceases to be a child of God.[19]

Although May's spirit was gentler than Garrison's, their opinions were very similar, at least until May moved to Syracuse, New York, so that his contacts with his old friend became intermittent. May's first tract on slavery, published by Garrison and Knapp in 1832,[20] insisted that slavery ought to be immediately abolished. It called for the Colonization Society to be "extinguished"; proclaimed the guilt of New England for acquiescing in the domestic slave trade as well as in the continuance of slavery in the territories and in the District of Columbia; and maintained the right and duty of every lover of freedom to speak out, regardless of Southern protests, against the monstrous wrongs being inflicted upon two million Americans. Characteristically, however, he acknowledged that the practical measures recommended by the advocates of immediate abolition would involve a slow process of emancipation; that doubtless there were members of the Colonization Society who supported it for honorable motives; and that some sort of indemnification might even be made to "all who may be materially injured by the overthrow of that great institution which we have upheld among them."[21]

May, like Garrison, preached the doctrine of nonviolence. Both of them, for example, regretted that Elijah Lovejoy had violated Christian principles by a resort to physical force.[22] Like Garrison, May came to look upon the Constitution as a proslavery document that must be overthrown, although this was not his view at the outset.[23] Like Garrison, he refused to join the political abolitionists who supported the Liberty Party; the enslaved are to be redeemed, he said in 1845, "by moral, and not by political partisan instruments."[24] Eventually, however, the two men were found on opposite sides of the issue of political action, since May gave the opening prayer at one of the sessions of the Free Soil Convention at Buffalo in 1848, and urged the *Liberator* to "gratefully recognize, in the event . . . some evidence of progress."[25] He thought of himself, by that time, as in some sense mediating between Garrison (and the New England abolitionists) and Gerrit Smith (and the New York group), the separation between the two having come about in part over this issue. In 1856, when Garrison would do no more than express a preference for Fremont over Buchanan, May was vigorously urging antislavery men of all shades of opinion to vote for the Republican candidate.[26]

While May's abolitionist views were not popular among the Unitarians at large, he was never criticized as sharply as Parker was, nor did he feel anything like the same degree of alienation from his brethren. Part of the explanation, no doubt, is that his theological position was not a radical one. Furthermore, the fact that he had well placed Unitarian connections on both sides of the family, including several

Unitarian ministers, is not to be overlooked. There was a time, indeed, when one of his cousins was general agent of the Massachusetts Anti-Slavery Society, while another was secretary of the American Unitarian Association.[27] But the crucial factors in May's relationship to the other Unitarian clergy were his irenic spirit and sweetness of disposition. The one occasion when it was widely felt that he overstepped the bounds of propriety was in 1851, when he offered a resolution at the Unitarian meetings in Boston condemning the Fugitive Slave Law, the preamble of which singled out a number of Unitarians by name as supporters of the law. The list included Dr. Gannett and Dr. Dewey, as well as political figures like President Fillmore and Daniel Webster. Dr. Gannett in particular was much hurt, but May argued that he had used the names to identify clearly and unambiguously the opinions he was condemning, and that he had not applied any opprobrious language to the men involved. But the editor of the *Christian Inquirer,* presumably Samuel Osgood, probably spoke for most of the Unitarian clergy when he chided May for "this first effort ever made among Unitarians to connect personalities with their deliberations." For May, he said, "we have been accustomed to entertain great respect"; he found it hard to reconcile May's action with "his character for good temper and sobriety."[28]

May's most active service in the abolition cause was in the period from 1830 to 1842. When he became principal of the Lexington Normal School in the latter year, Horace Mann insisted that he regard his duties there as having first call on his time, and even reprimanded him on one occasion for taking his students to a Sunday antislavery meeting in Waltham. After moving to Syracuse, May did not cease his antislavery lecturing, but had less occasion for time-consuming organizational activity. At no time, however, did he allow his antislavery activities to cripple his parish work, and he never felt any conflict of loyalties between his denominational connection and the cause of abolition. "I am as much of a Unitarian as ever," he declared, "as much of a Unitarian as I am of an Abolitionist."[29] Influence is not easy to measure; yet it well may be that it was men like May and James Freeman Clarke, rather than men like Theodore Parker and Thomas Wentworth Higginson, who were most effective in leavening the whole lump of the Unitarian clergy, so far as the great issue of that generation was concerned.

III

If Samuel J. May is to serve as the type of the Unitarian abolitionist, Henry W. Bellows of New York may serve to exemplify the moderate antislavery preacher. In his antislavery, as in his doctrinal preaching, Bellows was very much a middle-of-the-roader, trying to encompass as much as possible of the positions of those on both sides of him, sympathizing at least partially with each in turn, without identifying himself with any extreme. He had a good word to say about the abolitionists on more than one occasion, especially when others were attacking them. But he would characteristically couple praise with blunt criticism, or conversely, temper his criticism with a hearty acknowledgment that unpopular prophets are needed to keep the line of march on the move. He was equally quick, however, to defend Orville Dewey from abolitionist attacks, even though Dewey took a position on the Fugitive Slave Law for which he himself had no sympathy.

Bellows's contemporaries were often puzzled by his apparent inconsistencies. One observer, in 1859, described him as "a strange mixture of dispassionate argument and impulsive enthusiasm; a devotee in prayer, and a jovial companion in society; a radical and a conservative, a democrat and an aristocrat, a transcendentalist and a churchman, a man of the world and an evangelist."[30] Part of the explanation was doubtless his capacity to be inclusive in his sympathies, to understand the tragic dilemma of the conscientious slaveholder as well as the righteous concern of the abolitionist, to acknowledge that the preservation of the Union as well as the cause of human freedom might legitimately claim one's loyalty. His friend Cyrus Bartol saw him as essentially the mediator, the harmonizer, the reconciler of divergent views. He was aboard to trim the ship, to redress the balance whenever it listed too far on either side. Bellows had no notion, Bartol declared, "of letting any enterprise he was embarked in, by following extreme counsels, or by any exclusive tendency, go to excess."[31]

Bellows had, furthermore, a great gift for leadership, of an essentially charismatic quality. "But at times I will confess to you," he wrote to Bartol in 1848, at the age of thirty-four, "I have felt myself called to a more than common place in the world, to possess a more than ordinary discernment & to be capable of a wider & more permanent influence." While bothered by inner doubts as to whether he had sufficient originality or steadiness of purpose, he nevertheless felt "a sort of confidence that there was something in me which would one day come out & enable me to do a substantial & abiding work for mankind."[32] His effectiveness as a leader may well have been somewhat diminished by the abundance and variety of his enthusiasms; yet people did respond. They helped him to rebuild his own parish in the 1840s, to save Antioch College in the 1850s, to create the Sanitary Commission in the dark days of the Civil War, and to reconstruct the Unitarian denomination after 1865. He was a man of many projects and enormous energies; but more important, he was the kind of man who could enlist the support of others to do things that no man could do alone.

But the last thing in the world that Bellows could bear to be was a leader without any followers. He could take a stand for principle, even when it was unpopular with his people; but he would never do it in such a way as to cut himself off from them or jeopardize his chances of influencing them. Early in March, 1850, a committee of his church in New York waited on him, and requested him not to deliver a scheduled address on American slavery, but he would not yield to their pressure.[33] At the same time, he defended Dr. Samuel Gilman of the church in Charleston, who had come under criticism by his northern colleagues for his prudent silence on the slavery question. "To speak of slavery as it deserves, and as we are able to speak of it in New York, would require in Charleston an amount of candor, courage, and disinterestedness, positively sublime. And perhaps, what can be usefully said here, could not be usefully said there."[34]

How he sought to exert his influence in the parish Bellows pointed out in 1855 in a refreshingly candid letter, in which he declined to speak at an abolitionist meeting. There are two kinds of people interested in the antislavery cause, he suggested. There are those "who make it the business of their lives, and who take it up as the Apostles took up the Gospel, determined to know nothing else"; but then there are those "who make it subsidiary to other interests and aims, and urge and sustain it only as those other interests and aims allow." He rejoiced in the existence of the first class even though he belonged to the second and, for reasons entirely satisfactory to himself, intended to stay there. "I am a preacher of the Gospel," he explained, "a pastor, the head of a religious congregation." There were certain things he hoped to accomplish for the guidance and instruction of his flock. "Nothing can persuade me," he went on, "that it is pusillanimity, time-serving, the love of money or place, that restrains me from shocking, angering, and dispersing them by statements on any subject wholly beyond their sympathies." He was confident that he had planted right sentiments on the subject of slavery in the hearts of many, perhaps most, of his congregation, and he hoped with prudence to do more. "All the action of a more direct sort in behalf of the Anti-Slavery Cause, which my more binding duties as a pastor allow, I avail myself of just as fast as prudence justifies it—and beyond that justification, I shall neither be tempted nor driven."

There is a distinction in function, he concluded, between prophets and pastors. "Prophets address communities; pastors, flocks; prophets cry aloud and spare not; pastors give milk to babes, and meat to strong men; prophets obey a divine madness; pastors follow the rule of common sense and sober discretion." Every age has need of both, and he rejoiced "that prophets have been raised up to testify against the sin of Slavery—who have forgotten everything but their clear office to blow the trumpet against the walls of the doomed city." But he did not belong to their ranks. "It is only when the pastor's and the prophet's duties run together," he declared, "that I can temporarily occupy the prophet's place, and then only haltingly and in second-rate style—as a *minor* prophet indeed."[35]

Bellows's own congregation included many whose commercial interests linked them closely to the South. Perhaps, therefore, it was his own sense of ministerial prudence that held him back until the late 1840s from a vigorous public expression of the antislavery position to which he had long adhered. To be sure, in 1842 he praised Channing for his antislavery writings and argued that he had done more to destroy "this great wrong" than all the antislavery societies put together. Yet in 1845 Bellows's name was not among the signers of the "Protest Against American Slavery," which was circulated among all the Unitarian ministers and received the support of 170 of them. For his failure to sign he was chided by George F. Simmons, his contemporary at the Divinity School, who was greatly troubled because so few of the very prominent Unitarian ministers had been willing to take their stand on what was, after all, a pretty moderate antislavery platform. "Why did not you sign it?" Simmons inquired, almost plaintively. "Did not you believe? or did not you hope? or is it prudence? or do you reckon the matter not in your sphere? . . . Write me, & not as to an examining abolition committee, but as to a friend who is jealous of your character as he is jealous of his own."[36]

After the Mexican War, however, which Bellows opposed, the time seemed right for a more outspoken antislavery witness. His position from that time until the firing on Fort Sumter was a free-soil one. An editorial in the *Christian Inquirer* in 1849 indicates sufficiently well the position that Bellows was to restate on many occasions throughout the decade that followed. Slavery, he insisted, was an evil without qualification, but unfortunately one that has been placed beyond the legislative reach of the national government. "We are bound to abide by the constitution, until we have legal power to change it." As soon as we have that power, "we are bound to use it to undo whatever folly, former ignorance, haste, or wickedness led us into. Whenever there is a constitutional way of abolishing slavery in this Union, it ought to be done."[37] In the meantime, liberty, not slavery, must be the national policy; the extension of slavery must be prevented; the selfish indifference and apathy Northerners feel towards a distant evil must be ended; and once these things have been accomplished, the mobilized force of opinion may be relied upon to do the rest.

The one occasion when Bellows came closest to alienating at least an influential segment of his congregation was in 1850, when he condemned Webster's Seventh of March Address. He described the situation to Bartol:

> In this community, the commercial view of Slavery prevails, & is to be withstood. My views are not ultra—but I maintain the necessity not only of no compromise, but of an *avowed intention* to change the constitution by constitutional means, as soon as we have the power.

As for Webster, Bellows declared himself "grieved" and "shocked" by the failure of the speech to rise above the level of base expediency. "Mr. Webster has disgraced himself—I think—*ruined* himself by his politic bid for the Presidency."[38] A somewhat more discreetly phrased, but nonetheless unambiguous, criticism soon appeared in the editorial column of the *Christian Inquirer,* which Bellows had founded and was then editing.[39] This was followed in turn by a meeting of the directors of the Unitarian Association of the state of New York, the organization sponsoring Bellows's weekly newspaper, at which their dissatisfaction was placed in the form of resolutions to be transmitted to the editor. It was in the midst of this turmoil that Bellows insisted on delivering an antislavery address, as previously noted, despite the request of influential members of his congregation that he maintain a prudent silence. As Bellows reported to Bartol:

> For the past fortnight I've had a dreadful buzz about my ears. Trustees officially entreating silence. Proprietors of Inquirer passing votes of conscience &c—and I poor conscience-ridden man unable to oblige or give heed to any of them. It will come out right I suppose. I am apt to light on my feet even in the boldest jumps; but this is the first time I have had any serious trouble with my people.[40]

Two years later, Bellows preached a sermon on the death of Webster in which that statesman's errors, if such they were, were allowed to be forgotten, and he was eulogized as "the last of our great men." It is a fearful thing, Bellows exclaimed, "to remember that the powerful brake which the wisdom, moderation, and weight of that great statesman afforded is suddenly wrenched from the train!"[41] Yet there was a substantial difference between the two men. For one thing, Bellows refused to take as seriously as Webster did the threat of southern secession. "Every day is proving that the Union is in no danger," he wrote in 1850. "That threat has lost its power."[42] Thus Bellows avoided the poignant conflict of ideals that tormented his friend Orville Dewey, who felt that he had to yield on the issue of the Fugitive Slave Law for the sake of the Union. Bellows thought, almost down to the firing on Sumter, that the worst that could happen would be that one or two states might be foolhardy enough to try to secede, but that most of the slaveholding states would realize that they had at least as much at stake as did the North in the preservation of the Union. Any attempt at secession would therefore prove abortive.

Furthermore, while Bellows cherished the Union, he was ready to run the risk of disunion rather than permit the extension of slavery. He therefore vigorously supported Fremont and Dayton in 1856. Union, he said in a sermon just before the election, "is great, precious, sacred! but . . . humanity, duty, honor, religion . . . *are greater than the Union.*"[43] Because of this sermon, Thomas Wentworth Higginson invited him to participate in the disunion convention at Worcester early in 1857, but Bellows quickly set him straight on that issue. Disunion, he explained, is a danger to be risked, not a policy to be embraced. "Slavery and Freedom cannot live permanently together; and this is the reason why the North and South should—that the Liberty of the one may extinguish the Slavery of the other."[44]

But when the final accounting was called for, in April 1861, it was neither the issue of slavery nor the preservation of the Union that was controlling so far as Bellows was concerned. He saw no legal or moral justification for using force to end slavery in the South; and he would have been willing, in January 1861, to let the fifteen slaveholding states leave the Union in peace, had he thought they unitedly desired it. But he denied that the sentiment for secession in the South approached anything like unanimity, even though secessionists had gained control of the machinery of government in several of the Southern states. The problem, as he saw it in the anxious last days of the Buchanan administration, was not freedom versus slavery, or even Union versus secession, but social order versus disintegration and anarchy, precipitated by secessionist cliques. The firm exercise of the authority of the Federal government was the only "dignified, safe, constitutional, and Christian" way of dealing with "politicians, factions, schemers, conspirators." He stated his position epigrammatically thus: "Great revolutions must, in modern times, be made peaceful revolutions; little revolutions must be instantly quenched."[45] As soon, therefore, as Sumter was fired on, Bellows declared it "a matter of direst and most pressing necessity, to spring with united hearts and determined hands to the defence of the law and the maintenance of national authority."[46]

IV

A third category of antislavery minister, actually rather small in numbers, is represented by Orville Dewey, from 1835 to 1849 the minister of the Church of the Messiah in New York. Deeply concerned for the preservation of the Union and constitutional processes, he sought the containment and gradual abolition of slavery within that framework. Persuaded that Southern threats of secession were more than bravado and bluster, he accepted the compromise of 1850, deeming the Fugitive Slave Law a lesser evil than disunion. His willingness to go along with Webster on this issue readily distinguishes him from his close friend Bellows. Needless to say, he was bitterly condemned by the abolitionists, who held him up to scorn as no better than an apologist for the South. An extreme but not isolated instance is a reference to him as a "recreant, negro-hunting priest," who had "fouled his pulpit and disgraced his profession, by his advocacy of the Fugitive law . . ."[47]

Although Dewey did not sign the protest of the Unitarian ministers against slavery in 1845, he had not been silent on the issue. At an early date he had been a member of the Colonization Society, and possibly another antislavery group as well.[48] In a Thanksgiving sermon in 1837, he acknowledged that he was no abolitionist, but made it clear that he was no apologist for slavery either. "Slavery is," he declared, "undoubtedly, an anomaly in our free institutions"; he referred to it as a temporary though lamentable exception to the principle of freedom.[49] In 1844, he opposed the annexation of Texas,[50] which he regarded as no better than a proposal for legalized theft; while, in 1847, he agreed with the principle of the Wilmot Proviso, which would have forbidden the extension of slavery into territory being acquired from Mexico. Indeed, at that time he was fearful that northerners might compromise their principles in the face of southern threats of secession. For his part, he was ready to "take the risk of any consequences whatever" rather than "yield the national sanction to this huge and monstrous wrong."[51]

Dewey's opposition to slavery was based on certain theological assumptions about human nature and human destiny that were very similar to those of Channing, whose assistant he had once been. In a sermon entitled "The Slavery Question," preached in 1847, he declared that the controlling question was: "Are these people men?" If so, it is intolerable that they should be denied the opportunity for intellectual and moral growth. "It *cannot possibly be right* so to hold down and bind to earth the faculties of an immortal creature!"[52] Dewey felt that a period of tutelage would doubtless be necessary, and his early contact with the colonization movement seems to have led him to take it for granted that a separation of the races would be desirable, perhaps by turning over California to the Negroes that they might form an independent republic.[53] But the important thing to his mind was for the wealth and energies of the country to be devoted at once to preparing the slave for the freedom that was rightfully his.

Dewey's refusal to condemn the slaveholder categorically led abolitionist Unitarians to regard him as a trimmer in the 1840s, and his position on the Fugitive Slave Law laid him open to scornful and indeed vituperative attack. He was singled out in the Unitarian ministerial debates on slavery in 1851 as "more earnest and emphatic than any man in his asseveration that this law, infernal as it is, ought nevertheless to be obeyed."[54] He himself felt that he had been grievously misrepresented, and indeed, his position on this issue was so complicated and involved that it is easy to see how he could have been misunderstood. Much of the discussion centered on the question of whether he had actually said, as had been reported, that he "would sell his own mother into slavery rather than have the law violated." The Reverend Charles C. Shackford expressed a readiness to testify in a court of law that he had heard Dewey say it. The Reverend Robert C. Waterston insisted, rather, that Dewey had mentioned selling his own son into slavery.[55] Though a mild-mannered man, Dewey could with difficulty restrain himself from calling his accusers liars. After all, he had the manuscript text of his lecture, which demonstrated quite plainly that he had never suggested selling his mother into slavery or, for that matter, selling anyone into slavery. What he had said was something rather different: "I would consent that my own brother, my own son, should go (*i.e.* into slavery)—*ten times rather* would I go myself—than that this Union should be sacrificed for me or for us."[56] The language was doubtless excessively hyperbolic; but the image behind it was that of a Socrates accepting unjust punishment rather than escape, and not the slave trader trafficking in human lives.

Dewey thoroughly abhorred all fugitive slave laws, including the one of 1850, but he argued that such a law was part of the compact by which the nation had come into being and so it would have to be respected. Unless the North was prepared to make a crusade on the South in order to free the slaves by force, it would have to permit the slaveholder to recover fugitives. Dewey thought that the South would be well advised not to exercise its constitutional rights in the matter, and that it should look upon the law as a way of discouraging slaves from escaping, rather than as a mechanism for their recovery. But if there were no such law, what would happen? The North would be an asylum for fleeing slaves, and southerners would come north to try to find, seize, and return their property by force. Violence and inflamed feelings would inevitably result. It is far better, Dewey argued, to control this potentially dangerous and lawless situation with established procedures. The Fugitive Slave Law does not make slave catchers of northerners; what it does is put a restraining hand on southerners, and protect the putative slave until the southerner has proved his claim. What is the meaning of the legal procedure under the law? Dewey asked. "I understand it to be this. We will not let irresponsible persons come into our territory and seize whom they will, and bear him off to bondage. If you claim my man as owing you service, you must prove that he *is* the man you say he is, and not another."[57] The argument was a specious one, in view of the way in which the actual provisions of the law were weighted against the fugitive, and Dewey was naive to have swallowed it. But he was speaking in 1852, before the Anthony Burns case dramatically demonstrated how easily proceedings under the law might be manipulated so as to "legally" kidnap a free Negro into slavery.

Dewey was not the first moderate to find that he was under attack from two directions. He spent the winter of 1855–56 in Charleston, South Carolina, where he found congenial friends. The following summer, however, an address of his in which he reiterated his long-standing free-soil principles was brought to the attention of his Southern acquaintances, almost all of whom promptly broke off all relationships with him.[58] As the crisis of 1861 approached, his voice was heard in patriotic appeals for support of the Union;[59] and after the firing on Sumter, he spoke of the war as "a holy war," not for the abolition of slavery, but for the principle of Union and lawful sovereignty.[60]

V

The adverse judgment that has often been made on the moderates, referred to above, has usually been a reflection of the position taken by the abolitionists, and by Samuel J. May in particular, since his *Recollections* has frequently been relied on by historians. May was especially critical of Unitarian moderates because he was a Unitarian himself and felt that the humane theology professed by the liberals, together with the example of Channing, should have borne more abolitionist fruit. Since, apart from Garrison himself, the leaders of the Massachusetts

Anti-Slavery Society were chiefly Unitarians, May could never quite make up his mind whether he should praise the Unitarians for what they had done for the abolitionist cause, or castigate them for not having done more.

The easy explanation for the moderate position of most of the clergy on the slavery issue is that the commercial interests of Boston and New York had too great a stake in stable trade relationships with the South to be willing to permit agitation, and that the ministers could do no other than reflect the opinions of the pews. This kind of analysis is not irrelevant, since every responsible minister does his best to understand what his people are thinking and feeling; but it is obviously oversimplified, since there is evidence of repeated instances when ministers discovered that they were having difficulty carrying their congregations with them to an explicit condemnation of slavery.

No doubt there were ministers whose highest achievement was to accommodate their views to the established opinions of their people. Rightly or wrongly, Bellows thought of Dr. George Putnam of Roxbury as just such a man: "His chosen business seems to be to *justify what is,* & to give the existing feelings & opinions & purposes of the community back to it, in a religious nomenclature."[61] Yet most of the ministers would clearly have rejected such a concept of their role. They considered it to be their duty to mold opinion, not merely to reflect it. But they also regarded it as their duty to minister to their congregations with love and understanding, regardless of whether the members were abolitionist, moderate, or apathetic.

The simplest solution for a minister in such a situation is to take a stand for principle, even if it alienates a large fraction of the congregation, and to remake what remains in his own image; if the minister in a given case was above all an abolitionist, he would end up ministering to an antislavery society and not a church. But the great bulk of the clergy, including men like Samuel J. May, preferred another and more difficult course; and how successful they were depended more than anything else on the warmth and inclusiveness of their human sympathies, and on the wisdom and maturity with which they handled the problem of divergent views within their parishes. Even the ablest of them were not always able to prevent differences of opinion from leading to the disaffection of segments of their congregations. Yet, if we are to pass judgment on them at all, it must surely be not simply in terms of the extent to which they adhered to some given standard of antislavery orthodoxy, but in terms of their effectiveness in bringing their congregations to an increased awareness of the greatest moral issue confronted by that whole generation of Americans.

HENRY W. BELLOWS AND THE ORGANIZATION
OF THE NATIONAL CONFERENCE

The organization of the United States Sanitary Commission was Henry W. Bellows's greatest public service, and the one for which he is best remembered today. The organization of the National Conference in 1865, and his leadership in its affairs until his death in 1882, was his most important service to the Unitarian denomination. The exact nature and significance of this contribution to the Unitarian cause has been largely forgotten, however, with the result that the Unitarian debt to Bellows is not generally recognized. Furthermore, the story of the founding of the National Conference has never been told with full attention to the wealth of detail revealed in Bellows's own papers. The role he played has been seen, for the most part, through the eyes of the "radicals" of that day, who were unsympathetic with his objectives, reluctant participants in his projects, and willing critics of his successes. While the disaffection of men like Octavius Brooks Frothingham and Edward C. Towne is part of the story of those years, it is not necessarily the most significant part of it. Nor can one understand the renewed vitality of Unitarianism after two decades of stagnation if one relies chiefly on Towne's *ex parte* account of the organizing convention in New York in 1865. Between Bellows and his critics there is a balance yet to be struck, and much of the evidence is available in the Bellows Papers, in the custody of the Massachusetts Historical Society.[1]

I

In 1865, Bellows was at the height of his career. For more than twenty-five years he had been the minister of the Church of All Souls in New York, to which he had come as a young man, recently graduated from

the Harvard Divinity School. Twice already his congregation had outgrown its house of worship and had built anew. The range of his influence in Unitarian circles was extended by the *Christian Inquirer,* the
weekly religious newspaper he founded in 1847, for which he wrote
constantly. In the life of New York City, he had assumed a prominent
role, both as a religious and as a civic leader. In the antislavery movement he had led his congregation to an increasingly advanced position
without becoming an extremist. In the secession crisis of 1861 he had
helped to mobilize Union sentiment. In 1865, he was fifty years of age;
his natural powers were vigorous and undiminished; his confidence in
his ability to enlist men in the willing and enthusiastic support of good
causes was sustained by his undoubted successes in the Sanitary Commission; his contacts with men of consequence throughout the country
were far-reaching; his reputation was a commanding one.

   During the course of the war, Bellows had become convinced that
new tides of popular feeling were beginning to surge through the country, that old theological formulations were crumbling, and that the
churches were entering a period of flux from which new patterns and
alignments were likely to emerge. A new sense of American nation-
ality had developed, and Americans had been brought into new relationships with one another. Nonsectarian philanthropic activity like that
of the Sanitary Commission had broken down walls of denominational
exclusiveness. The doctrine of human dignity had been vindicated in
the abolition of slavery. Soldiers facing death on the field of battle had
been thrust back to the foundations of religious faith, and away from
theological debate and sectarian polemic. The actual faith by which
men were living was no longer represented for them by the creeds of
evangelical Christianity. As a result, Bellows argued, millions of Americans had become "thoroughly undermined in the foundation of the
faith of their parents"; they were "trying to find some substitute in
ethics or pseudo or real science, for a religion in which they cannot
longer believe."[2]

   In such a situation, in which sectarian lines were being shaken and
the "crust of ecclesiastical and theological usage" had been broken up
"as the ice is broken by the spring freshet,"[3] Bellows saw an opportunity for the Unitarians to become for the first time a denomination
with national influence. His conviction that this was the case was reinforced in the Spring of 1864, when he went to California to assist the

San Francisco church after the untimely death of Starr King, and saw openings there for Unitarian advance on all sides, awaiting only vigorous and sustained missionary activity. "The attractions of this field are great & almost irresistible," he wrote home:

> There is much to be done which *can be done!* It is like furnishing a new house when you have the money in hand! You cant keep your hands off the new carpets, they cry so to be tacked down! All things are possible here. . . . Liberal Christianity has taken new root, & movements to multiply our Churches on this coast are fairly under hopeful consideration. I shall be disappointed if, a year hence, there are not five or six Unitarian Societies on foot.[4]

Bellows was not one to see a job to be done and shirk his own responsibility in the matter. Early in 1864, he wrote to Edward Everett Hale:

> As soon as the War is over, there will be a chance for great doings. . . . I hope to live to take an active part—when the [Sanitary Commission] is off my hands,—in this new Reformation, which will like a good householder bring forth things *new* & *old,* in its Church-life & creed.[5]

Towards the end of 1864, when preliminary planning for the New York convention had begun, he wrote even more pointedly to his son:

> I have a buoyant hope that we are on the verge of a grand revolution in the theological & religious views of Society & that *now* is the day & hour for great undertakings in our Body. . . . I feel as if my Sanitary work had been only a providential discipline & preparation for this still nobler & more imperative undertaking.[6]

Although opportunities for denominational growth were developing in many areas, it was uncertain whether the Unitarians would be able to take advantage of them. Ever since Emerson's Divinity School Address in 1838, and more particularly since Parker's South Boston Sermon in 1841, serious tensions had existed within the denomination. The more conservative wing was insistent that Christianity was of divine origin and sanction and that Jesus Christ, though not a person of the Trinity, was divinely authorized to proclaim the way of salvation to erring men. At the other extreme the "radicals"—as they were coming to call themselves—were moving towards a wholly naturalistic interpretation of religion, which allowed no specially privileged place for Jesus. Emerson had referred to the tendency of historic Christianity to dwell "with noxious exaggeration" on the person of Jesus. By way of reaction against traditional Christian piety quite as much as against orthodox Christian doctrine, some radicals had developed an extremely negative response to even the most liberal interpretation of the personality of Jesus. But to the extent that Unitarianism was becoming polarized this way, it was also becoming paralyzed, and support for the Unitarian Association was diminished. "This outbreak, if I may call it so, of Mr. Parker," insisted Samuel K. Lothrop, "disintegrated the clergy and the whole body of Unitarians. . . . Since then the Unitarian Congregationalists as a body have never been a unit, as they were during the first forty years of this century."[7] In Lothrop's comment, there is a suggestion that Parker was somehow personally to blame for the failure of Unitarianism to retain its earlier momentum. But one does not have to accept that implication to acknowledge the essential validity of his judgment. There seems to be good reason to believe that financial support of missionary activities had been adversely affected by divisions within the Unitarian body.[8]

Historians have generally ranked Bellows with the conservative wing of the denomination.[9] But it was never his way to adhere to any extreme position, whether of the right or of the left, if it were possible to find a middle ground. "I am I believe on both sides of all great questions," he wrote in 1863, "because truth rides a-*horse-back;* her limbs are invisible to each other & in opposite stirrups, but her trunk is one."[10] He acknowledged that he often found himself in difficulties because of his readiness to treat half the truth, for the time being, as the whole truth, reserving for another occasion the counterbalancing half. But the role of mediator was the one for which he was temperamentally fitted, and he chose it consciously:

> I have endeavored to bring into our own Denomination, the elements which sectarian antagonisms had for a time excluded. . . . I have sought deliberately to be on *both sides* of the theological, the political & the social questions of the day, endeavoring to do a reconciling & an impartial work, in a spirit of love & charity. This has often subjected me to charges of vacillation & changeableness, among those who merely saw the pendulum now in one & now in another portion of its arc, without observing the fixed centre from which it swings so freely.[11]

But the friends who knew him best understood him for what he was: an inveterate middle-of-the-roader, who sought always to draw the extremes closer together. Bartol's comment after his death was a just one:

> Accordingly, his talent, his temper, was to mediate, harmonize, reconcile. He admitted he was on board to trim the ship, to unfurl or reef the sail, to roll the heavy, iron-laden car on trucks from side to side of the main deck to keep from careening and maintain an even keel. To what was peculiar and sometimes seemed inconsistent in his position, this was the key. He had no notion of letting any enterprise he was embarked in, by following extreme counsels, or by any exclusive tendency, go to excess.[12]

If the Unitarians were to survive, Bellows felt, the conservatives and radicals would both have to be brought closer to a middle ground, if not in theology, at least in their willingness to cooperate in common endeavors. But more than that, the Unitarian body as a whole would have to be persuaded to organize more effectively, to take seriously the problem of creating the kind of institutional structures that would enable free men to consolidate their efforts and do together what they could never do separately. Doubtless it was Bellows's experience in the Sanitary Commission that had sharpened his vision of what might be achieved. In the organization of scores of local auxiliaries, in the collection of money by sustained solicitation and subscription, in the detailed planning that was necessary for the popular and successful Sanitary Fairs, Bellows had learned how much could be done by the voluntary efforts of men and women mobilized by able leaders in the service of a great cause. It was a similar vision of the possibilities of Liberal Christianity that he had glimpsed, and it was a comparable method of organization that seemed to him the way to success. After the Civil War, the development of industrial society in America meant that the forms of effective human association would involve larger units in many fields—business, government, and labor most obviously. Several of the religious denominations likewise began to develop new forms of national organization. Among Unitarian leaders, Bellows was the one who saw most clearly that his own denomination would also have to develop new institutional forms, with a national scope and vision, in which the laity would have to participate actively.

For this kind of constructive enterprise, the Unitarians were singularly ill prepared. They had inherited the most parish-oriented version of New England congregationalism, which had always shunned regularly established extra-parochial structures. Doubtless this had mattered little in colonial times when the population was only just beginning to be religiously pluralistic and when state support of the Standing Order provided the churches with a structure to which they could attach themselves in the absence of ecclesiastical relationships. But even when times had changed, when society had become pluralistic and the Standing Order was gone, Unitarians continued to be narrowly parochial. It was assumed that churches that had survived for two hundred years with no formal organization for cooperative endeavor would continue to survive without it, and that new churches would somehow spring up on their own with no need for intervention on the part of the older ones. Hence the refusal of many old-line Unitarians in the first half of the nineteenth century to acknowledge that there could be any legitimate kind of denominational organization, their frequent rejection of the Unitarian name, and their halfhearted support of the American Unitarian Association, even though this was no more than a voluntary association of individual subscribers.

Bellows feared that it would take an enormous effort to overcome parochialism and apathy on the part of the conservative wing. "I see nothing but sure decay for our cause, in the sybaritic sloth, the Sadducean skepticism, the contented respectability, that now clothes its older members," he wrote to Hale.[13] The men he had in mind are easy to identify. They were the older Boston ministers, whom he characterized thus:

> *The elder men*, old fashioned Unitarians, very *ethical* in their humor—preaching the doctrine of self-culture & personal righteousness. This part is identified with Boston respectability, & is opposed to all *vulgar publicity* & popular methods of arousing attention. Moreover it is very Congregational—sticklers for individual independence in the churches, and very little disposed to expect great things, or to undertake large enterprises. It is conservative too, & very spiteful towards the transcendental or radical wing, and pretty jealous of any thing which dont originate in Boston. I think Dr. Gannett may be considered as the head of this section, & George Ellis, Lothrop, Thompson, Hill, of Worcester are specimens of it.[14]

Mentioned separately by Bellows, though the distinction may seem to us excessively refined, is what he called a *"small section* of Evangelicals . . . of whom Rufus Ellis, Mr. Sears & a very few others are samples." These men, he believed, "want to *secede* & are disposed to deny any fellowship with the looser & more liberal party."[15]

In Bellows's view, the chief problem with the Boston ministers was that they had a truncated doctrine of the Church: "Is not the notion of *the Church* as distinct from the Churches, pretty much lost out of the N-Eng^d consciousness? especially out of the Unitarian consciousness?" But if the Boston conservatives had a limited and parochial concept of the Church, the radicals were in worse shape, because they had almost none at all. "I feel a dreadful *thin*ness in the philosophy & phrasing of my dear Bartol," Bellows went on to say.[16] Radicalism might be intellectually alive and stimulating, but it seemed to have little corporate vitality. The truth is, Hale complained, "that the extreme left is very apt to select for itself a lazy sort of life—stepping out occasionally to lecture or to supply a vacant pulpit—but turning up its philosophical nose at the routine of the organization of a parish."[17] Rationalism, or radicalism, Bellows was persuaded, "is *not a working power,* even at its *livest* state"; he predicted that the young men, "noble & earnest as many are," would find this out "when they attempt *work* on a grand scale—outside the little field of N. Eng. where what comes up is due to the general husbandry of the past, more than to the labors of the present farmer."[18]

The Boston conservatives stood for congregational self-sufficiency; this gave them strong local churches but limited horizons. The radicals stood for individual self-sufficiency and freedom; this gave them "churches of two, churches of one,"—sometimes considerable intellectual vigor, but no viable institutional structures to assure survival. "These men are shy of Convention," Bellows commented, "thinking some test may be applied, some creed slipped round them. They take alarm at any suggestion of any standard of faith—however generous, but are partly willing to co-operate on some platform of *Work* which has no doctrine in it."[19]

Bellows identified himself with neither the conservatives, nor the "evangelicals," nor the radicals, but with "Broad Church men" like Clarke, Hedge, and Hale. These men and numerous others, he declared, "recognize the elements of truth in all the other sections & believe in the possibility of welding them together . . ."[20] There is no hint either in letters or public statements of any desire to cut off either wing. Indeed, so far as the radicals were concerned, he seems to have had more respect for them than for the conservatives, despite his disagreement with their theology and with their extreme individualism.

"The real *life* in our body is in the *heretical* wing," he wrote to Hedge. "If we cut *it* off, there is nothing to move with!"[21]

Whether the middle party was large enough and strong enough to build on, Bellows felt, could only be discovered by making the attempt. Usually he was hopeful; sometimes he despaired of success; but in any event, it would be the extent to which the New York convention would draw support from all factions that would determine success or failure. Widespread apathy or deliberate refusal to participate would disclose the judgment of history, not simply on the convention, but on the Unitarian movement itself:

> It is to test our *virility*. We either *can* or *cant* propagate our species! If we are impotent, we are to show it, & make way for those who have the future in their loins. The sooner we are *known* to be as a Denomination, childless—"no son of ours succeeding," the sooner the throne of liberal Xty will pass into the hands of another Dynasty; & if we cant fill it—it is time it should. I fear our Brothers dont know what peril of being superseded we are in. Five years of our present apathy, divisions, & meditations on our own navel, will kill us sure—if we are not dead now. . . . So, be it successful or a failure, I'm equally interested in putting our cause to the test of this occasion.[22]

Yet the sensitivity of the radicals on the issue of intellectual freedom would pose a problem, as Bellows knew full well. No organized national religious movement could come into being, he was convinced, if it was unwilling to define for the public at large what its essential theological stance was to be. The new organization could not avoid some kind of doctrinal statement. Bellows struggled with the problem, which has proved to be a perennial one for Unitarians, of how to make a statement of belief that would be descriptive of the prevailing consensus without being limiting, that would mark out a distinctive part of the theological landscape which the Unitarians proposed to occupy without walling it in. At the outset, he assumed that some kind of creedal statement or "pronunciamento" was called for. But the language he used shows that he sought a unitive statement of opinion, not a definition of Unitarian orthodoxy that could be used to exclude nonconformists. In January 1865, he detailed to Hale what he had in mind:

> Now I dont expect to be able to *suit every body,* in any statement; &, let the unsuited drop—but cant we make a statement which will articulate the *actual* opinions of the vast majority of thotful Unitarians of both wings? It is not desirable that the creed should take the terms of

Science, or be in *stupid prose*. It should be somewhat mystic, & poetic in the true sense, addressed to the spiritual imagination; retaining the symbolism, but sloughing off the husks of the Church Universal (Historical). I think we might *boldly* design such a statement, which would be stable enough to stand on & fight with, & yet not so fenced in, & measurable with inch & foot lines, as to crowd out & alarm the free & the rational.[23]

Enough opposition to any such statement was promptly expressed in many quarters—and not merely by the radicals—for Bellows to conclude that discussion of the matter at the convention would be divisive rather than unifying.[24] He, therefore, dismissed the notion at least three weeks before the meeting assembled:

It is plain that what *I* desired in the way of a creed (without the objection of its binding authority) a creed that should show the continuity of the Christian consciousness to be in our body, & form the bridge *over* for those anxious to leave their present [straightened (?)] quarters, but *afraid* to come to *us*—is an idea for which our people are *not* prepared, & the value of which they dont understand. The discussion on that point is vastly better *out of Convention* than in it. *It has been discussed,* & plainly, the feeling & experience of the Body is *against* it. Let us abandon it then, altogether, in that form. . . . I think in place of a Christian symbol our people *are prepared for a practical statement* of our fundamental & distinctive ideas. . . .[25]

Bellows was willing to adopt a "practical" statement of purpose instead of a Christian creed or "symbol," but that does not mean that he proposed to abandon Christianity as the basis for the new organization. But the reason for his loyalty to the Christian tradition was not the usual one for that generation, and so the real point of difference between him and the radicals can easily be misunderstood. In the 1840s, conservative Unitarians like Andrews Norton had confronted the Transcendentalists with a rehearsal of Christian evidences, especially the miracles of Jesus, as the essential basis for belief in the divine origin and sanction of Christianity. Bellows in 1865 was not that kind of conservative; Christian evidences in the traditional sense had become peripheral in his thought. He had read Parker's *Discourse of Religion* and was not bothered by the concept of "Absolute Religion," which is the common possession of all men everywhere.[26] God, he readily acknowledged, is universally present, "in the world, in Nature, in your souls, everywhere."[27]

What he objected to in the Parkerites was not their characterization of cherished aspects of Christianity as transient expressions of absolute religion, but the fact that they undervalued the historical particularities through which we apprehend the Absolute. "It is very much like saying that because the *Sun* is the source of light & heat, we will give up fires on our hearths or gas & candles in our houses, & live out of doors."[28] People are not religious in general, Bellows seems to be saying, but are religious in a particular way as they participate in a present situation shaped by a particular historical tradition. It is the transient aspects of religion that require our care and attention, lest we be left with no religion at all. The church, in particular, is the instrument through which Christian contact with God has been sustained and made fruitful. So far as our relations with God and Christ "are not instituted, organized, methodized, they lack steadiness, force and influence." There are "natural sources of connection" with God and Christ; but "the church is the only unfailing, organized, direct connection with them, we have." Joining the church is not denying "that any life or power exists in reason, nature, literature, conscience, life to give [us] spiritual food; but only seeing that it is best to go where express, ample and constant provision is made by God to meet that great want."[29]

Bellows's insistence on a Christian basis for the National Conference, then, was not so much a defense of the supernatural claims of Christianity as it was an assertion that no substitute for the historic fact of the Christian church was available. Whatever might be said in an abstract, philosophical, timeless sense about Absolute Religion, human beings live here and now, and need the institutions that are relative to human wants and weaknesses. "We shant want Christianity in heaven, any more perhaps than the Bible—which we surely shant have. But we want it *now* prodigiously, both as the *public* Religion, and the private cultus."[30]

It is misleading, therefore, to see the disagreement between Bellows and the radicals—even though some of them doubtless did see it that way—as a simple conflict between conservative Christian confessionalism and a free religion unfettered by inherited intellectual dogmas or limits. What was controlling with Bellows was not Christian supernaturalism, though he accepted it, but a doctrine of the Church—that is to say, a concept of the nature and necessity of institutional religion. It was the fact that Bellows had a doctrine of the Church, while the radicals did not, that made the difference between them. The fact that he was Christian, while they were "naturalists," or "rationalists," or "free religionists," has to be understood in the context of that even more basic disagreement.

Bellows was never an ideologue who believed that salvation would be found in some perfectly thought-out theological or philosophical system. Practical results were too important to him; he was convinced that the way to get things done was by organizing the necessary institutions. If the acceptance of a particular ideology would lend strength and cohesion to an institution, well and good, but he was not inclined to sacrifice a necessary institution for the sake of maintaining some standard of ideological purity.

Since the denomination was, in fact, predominantly Christian, this was the obvious basis on which to start building. If the new enterprise was to grow by attracting disillusioned liberals from other Christian groups, all the more reason to erect a standard of liberal Christianity. If, as a consequence, some of the radicals developed scruples that would inhibit them from participating, however generously they might be invited, there was no reason why they should be either coerced or condemned. Bellows sincerely hoped that there would be few who would not go along, just as he hoped to draw in the Boston parochialists. But if any remained without, it should be by their own choice, not by any act of exclusion. "We want to describe a large eno' circle to take in all who really belong with us—and provided one, & the *fixed* leg of the compasses is in the heart of Jesus Christ I care very little how wide & far the other wanders."[31]

Of course Bellows was not alone in thinking that Unitarians would have to organize a new effort of wider scope to take advantage of new opportunities. Others may not have been as conscious as he of the whole range of possibilities, and did not project schemes that were as ambitious—even grandiose—as his, but they were nevertheless making similar criticisms and suggestions. Thus in an essay read to his ministerial brethren in the spring of 1864, James Freeman Clarke identified individualism as "our great foe," and complained that the "social and corporate element in our religious system is very weak."[32] At the annual meeting of the American Unitarian Association in May, the Reverend Carlton A. Staples spoke of the need for reorganizing missionary activity in the West, and he, like Bellows, argued that the influence of the War, and indeed the whole drift of events, had been favorable to liberal religion.[33] The same note was struck by the Reverend William J. Potter of New Bedford, whose address at the special meeting of the Association on December 7, 1864, may well have given Bellows some ideas for the elaboration of a theme that had already attracted him.[34] Bellows did not singlehandedly produce the ferment which had begun to stir in the denomination, but more than anyone else, he brought a variety of proposals into focus and into relationship to one another. It was his role to lay out a program of action, to enlist workers in the cause of a "new reformation," to be the tireless and eloquent spokesman for many who could not command the attention that he could, and to push through to some kind of permanent organization, more representative and hence more effective than the A.U.A.

II

The first formal step on the path that ultimately led to the New York convention was taken, not by Bellows, but by the executive committee of the Unitarian Association. Meeting in Boston on September 12, 1864, the committee was confronted with a severe financial crisis, and the president, Rufus P. Stebbins, was asked to prepare a special appeal for funds. A vote was also passed "to appoint a Committee of three to report some plan for increasing the usefulness of the Association . . ." Named to the committee, in addition to Stebbins, were the Reverend Charles Lowe, who was later to become the quietly tactful and efficient secretary of the Association, and Warren Sawyer, a layman from the Hollis Street Church.[35]

At the October meeting of the executive committee, the treasurer, Charles C. Smith, reported a deficit; a month later, as a temporary expedient, he was authorized to dip into capital. At the November meeting, also, the special committee, at Lowe's suggestion, proposed an extraordinary meeting of the Association on December 6 and 7, at which the whole financial problem should be explored. The plan was approved, and details entrusted to the special committee, now enlarged to include the treasurer and Henry P. Kidder, a Boston banker and an active member of Edward Everett Hale's church.[36]

The usual Autumnal Convention was not held in 1864, and so a large group was attracted to the special meeting, held at the Hollis

Street Church. Bellows came on from New York, having been particularly requested by Lowe to report on California in the hope of fostering increased financial support for the cause of Liberal Christianity.[37] On Tuesday evening, December 6, Rufus Stebbins spoke first, detailing the financial needs of the Association, the expedients that had been adopted for economical operation, the encouraging response to his special appeal that had begun to come from the churches, and the unmet calls on the limited funds of the Association. One suspects that Bellows felt these remarks to be too prudential and cautious, for when called upon to speak next in turn, he began by asserting that the work of the Association, though carried on with zeal and integrity, "was too small to satisfy our pride, moral ambition, or spiritual desires." In vivid language he went on to describe the work Starr King had begun in California, which now needed additional impetus; he outlined the needs of Meadville and Antioch; and he urged the formation, on a large scale, of an organization for missionary efforts in which the churches would be represented by both lay and ministerial delegates.

The following day, James P. Walker, a Boston layman whose publishing house specialized in Unitarian literature, spoke at length of the inadequate support the Association had received from the beginning. The average annual budget, as he computed it, had been only about $8,000. He proposed a financial drive to raise $25,000 for the current year and gradually increasing sums thereafter. Edward Everett Hale responded that the sum should be $100,000, and Walker's proposal was amended to that effect on motion by Henry P. Kidder. Bellows then declared that the crux of the matter was "the want of the proper machinery" for enlisting widespread and continuing support. He proposed a committee of ten persons, three ministers and seven laymen, to be charged with the responsibility for calling a convention in New York "to consider the interests of our cause and to institute measures for its good." The resolutions by Walker and Bellows were received with great enthusiasm, and were unanimously adopted. Needless to say, Bellows was named to head the committee, to which Hale was also appointed.[38]

Bellows deliberately suggested a committee on which laymen would be in a majority, because he was much concerned to secure their involvement in denominational affairs. One of his recurrent criticisms of the A.U.A. was that it was too much a clerical operation. Laymen of prominence and substance were chosen, with the obvious intent of giving prestige to the undertaking. They included Henry P. Kidder of Kidder, Peabody & Co.; A. A. Low of Brooklyn, merchant and financier; and Enoch Pratt of Baltimore, capitalist and philanthropist.[39] It was also no accident that the convention was to meet in New York, rather than Boston, and that only four of the members of the committee were from New England. One, Artemas Carter, was from as far away as Chicago. There was, nevertheless, some criticism from western ministers that none of their number had been included, and so Bellows afterwards added George W. Hosmer of Buffalo.[40]

Bellows wrote in detail to his son about the meeting in Boston:

> We had a special meeting of the American Unitarian Association, on Tuesday & Wed[y] of last week in Boston. Tuesday, I occupied pretty much the whole evening with an exposition of our interests on the Pacific Coast, with great interest on the part of the audience. Wednesday we debated the wants & prospects of our Unitarian cause. I bro't forward a scheme for reorganizing the whole denomination on a basis of *work*, & not of creed; argued the importance of a strictly representative organization, minister & two delegates from each parish, to legislate in a National Convention for the interests of the whole body; to raise large sums of money; to endow Antioch College; reanimate Meadville & stretch our cords over the Union, in a deliberate & powerful effort to meet the New Civilization & new public sentiment, developed by the War, by a Religion free, large, spirited & up to the times. I maintained that the time had come for a reanimation of our Liberal Xty & its appearance on the public Stage, in National proportions. It made a great Stir, was hailed by the young men with enthusiasm, by the middle-aged with Sympathy & offers of co-operation, & by the older ministers with *tacit acquiescence*. They did not support me openly or gladly, but were silent & non-committal. . . . I see a great future in it, & wish I had nothing else to do but to carry it out with a bold energy which would ensure success.[41]

So it was that the shaping of the denomination was placed largely in the waiting hands of Bellows—for it seems hard to accept as anything but a temporary aberration his comment to his son: "Our people are aroused & demand action, and I find myself in the post of leader, against my will & expectation."[42] Hale was, in effect, second in command, with special responsibility to talk up the convention among the Boston brethren. Of course, doubts and hesitation were expressed in some quarters. The Reverend Charles H. Brigham of Taunton was "sceptical about the practical worth of very large schemes for a body so small as ours," even though he had been named to the committee of ten,[43] and it was reported that Rufus Stebbins was beginning to wonder whether he had done the right thing in allowing the new movement to receive the sanction of the A.U.A. Bellows's leadership of it was apparently resented by some:

> It is very evident that there is a small, mean dissent from it, and un-willingness to enter heartily into it, on the part of a few men—I really believe that three fourths of this opposition proceeds from jealousy of Dr. Bellows. These men foresee that with his splendid gifts, his mag-netic speech, his royal personality and above all his magnificent devotion to great movements and ideas, he will naturally be the leader, the Head of the new regime. If this new movement succeeds he will be at the top of the new American Ecclesiasticism. This is a consummation most devoutly not wished for by a few men who have tried to be dictators but could not [get] anybody to accept their dictation.[44]

It should be kept in mind that, in the weeks that followed, both Bellows and Hale were concerned with many projects besides the New York convention. Bellows was attending regular meetings of the Board of the Sanitary Commission in Washington. Hale and he were con-sulting frequently with those involved in the selection of a new presi-dent for Antioch College, which they saw as a feeder for Meadville and hence an essential part of denominational strategy.[45] The *Christian Inquirer* needed a new editor; and Joseph Henry Allen, editor of the *Christian Examiner,* was negotiating for the transfer of the magazine to Bellows, so that it might be tied in with the new denominational organization.[46] Both Bellows and Hale were helping to raise the $100,000 for the A.U.A. voted on December 7.[47] And all of this was in addition to regular parish duties.

Nevertheless, Bellows summoned the committee of ten to meet at his home, 59 East 20th Street, on Wednesday, January 25; and Hale re-sponded to Bellows's request that he go on to New York ahead of time, to "cut & dry the business of the Committee the day before it meets."[48] The attendance on January 25 was all that could have been expected. Pratt was not present; Hosmer was prevented by illness; and Brigham had to be at an installation. But substitutes were found for Pratt and Brigham, so the committee was almost full.

One needs only to compare the letter Bellows wrote to Hale ten days before the meeting, outlining his views as to what had to be done, with the official report issued at its close, to realize the extent to which the chairman placed his own stamp on the proceedings. There seem to have been only a few points—such as the date for the convention to meet, which was set for April 5 and 6—for the committee to work through to a conclusion of its own.[49] On most matters, Bellows's advance preparation had laid out conclusions for the committee to ratify. It was at this particular stage in the development of plans for the convention that Bellows had the most elaborate notions of the kind of doctrinal statement, or "rallying-cry," the convention might adopt. He outlined his views in a prepared statement, which met with general approval. While its presuppositions were unambiguously Christian, and while it suggested the use of an abridged and thoroughly Unitarianized version of the Apostles' Creed, its main concern was to find common ground on which the largest possible number might stand. It would be impossible to draw a line through the Unitarian body, declared Bellows, without leaving men of equal worth on either side, nor could any group be cut off without losing "something vital, significant, and precious." Furthermore, the Liberal Christian Church of America, of which Bellows dreamed, would be expected to attract many restless believers out of orthodox churches who had never had any previous Unitarian connection. Therefore "no excision, denial of Christian standing, or refusal of fellowship, is to be encouraged in either direction, whether towards those leaning towards the old creeds, or those leaning towards Rationalism."[50]

For both Hale and Bellows, one measure of the success of the convention would be the number of churches represented and delegates, especially lay delegates, present. A convention which could win no more support than the A.U.A. had had would be, almost by definition, a failure. Hale wrote of the necessity "to lay out a plan, for approaching in advance each church of importance—& getting them to promise to be present."[51] A sermon delivered by Bellows to his own congregation was printed as a sort of campaign document,[52] and an official invitation, followed by an "Address to the Churches," went out early in February.[53]

Bellows was especially concerned about the response from parochial Boston. Hale reported that Dr. Gannett "saw difficulties unnumbered," but was nevertheless willing to attend with his two laymen.[54] Since Gannett was not at all well, this indicated genuine concern for the common cause, regardless of what Bellows may at times have said about Gannett's conservatism. Rufus Ellis, on the other hand, laid the question before the members of the First Church without recommendation, and was doubtless well content when they "voted thirty-nine to four not to send."[55] Hale was convinced that actually subtle pressure had been applied, and made sure that one hundred copies of Bellows's sermon were sent over to the First Church. "Young America in the parish was rampant," and kicked up a row, but to no avail.[56] At the Second Church, Chandler Robbins preached a sermon in which he stated that the Society had a right to vote as it saw fit on the matter, but that if the decision was to send, he would resign. His tactics were strongly resented by some members of the church, but his threat was nonetheless effective.[57]

Cyrus A. Bartol of the West Church was one of Bellows's oldest and most intimate friends and one whose presence he particularly sought. Bartol does not fit easily into any of the usual categories of Unitarian ministers of that generation. The West Church had a strong tradition of congregational localism which reinforced Bartol's intense, even exaggerated, transcendentalist concept of religion as a purely spiritual force. To go as an official representative of the West Church was out of the question; to go unofficially was an alternative about which he could not make up his mind, and until the very end he seemed likely to stay away. But Bellows told him there were two spare rooms in his house; one was for Hedge, the other would be for Bartol even if he did not make up his mind until the last minute. Friendship at last overcame scruples, and Bartol finally did attend, stayed as a house guest of Bellows, and observed the proceedings without participating. Bellows was grateful for his presence, even though Bartol returned home still affirming that the unseen harmony of the spirit was what really mattered, not visible cooperation in human institutions.[58]

Of the radicals, Octavius Brooks Frothingham presented the greatest problem, partly, one suspects, because Bellows and he were men of very different temperaments, who tended to irritate one another. Although Bellows was very likely unaware of it, Frothingham still nursed a grievance because Bellows had not attended the dedication ceremony at his new church on December 25, 1863. The story of that earlier episode is complicated and only indirectly relevant to the New York convention. Suffice it to say that a trivial matter involving a misunderstanding on both sides had left a lasting residue.[59]

Frothingham viewed the coming convention, in any event, with little satisfaction, and it seemed to Bellows that his negativism was doing damage to the cause. His attitude contrasted sharply with that of John White Chadwick, the other radical in the New York area, with whom Bellows always got along well.[60] Towards the end of February, Bellows got the impression that Frothingham did not mean to come in, and at that juncture, he rather hoped he would not.[61] But Frothingham could not help but feel the pressure of opinion, and at a ministers' meeting in Boston on March 14, he surprised everyone by his conciliatory tone. Hale had expected him to come "with a stiff attack on the Convention." Instead his address was "even deprecatory in its eagerness to avoid controversy"; he even went so far as to attempt a statement of consensus for the denomination "which if you took it without knowing who wrote it—would answer for one wing almost as well as for the other." Even this high point of Frothingham's willingness to cooperate was somewhat less than wholehearted, however, for he was heard to remark to Gannett: "If you will not attack me, I will not attack you."[62] The most that Frothingham would say in advance was that he did not intend to disrupt the proceedings:

> Frothingham professes great friendliness & tells me he intends no trouble & no division—"after Convention he will withdraw *if he dont like results*"—as every body will! Still, I dont think he knows his own mind eno' to be depended [on]. I think he means well, *just now,* towards the Convention, but is capable [of] bolting, or quarrelling, or contradicting [his] purpose at 15 minutes notice—[63]

By the middle of March, Bellows felt that representation of enough churches was assured to make the convention a success. "It is clear," he wrote to Hale, "that we shall have the weight of the Denomination in the Convention. Already the tide is turned, & is with the general ends & objects we seek."[64] His attention was now increasingly drawn to matters of detail. He had the kind of imagination that could picture precisely how he hoped things would go. He could scarcely restrain himself from writing James Freeman Clarke's keynote sermon for him, so that the right points would be made with just the right emphasis.[65] When Hale met with a group in Boston to work on the agenda, Bellows deluged him with detailed suggestions, not all of which, by any means, were accepted.[66]

Bellows had something to contribute at every point, even on the matter of local arrangements. If he dominated the proceedings, it was because he had thought through the details and had a plan, not because he expected to have his own way all the time. Indeed, his effectiveness as an organizer may be seen especially in the alert way in which he incorporated the usable ideas of others into his own plans. A. A. Livermore wrote to him to argue that a layman should preside, and to suggest the name of Governor John A. Andrew of Massachusetts. It was so arranged.[67] The *Christian Inquirer* suggested that the keynote sermon should be delivered on the evening before the business session opened, and that the recently vacated building of the Church of the Messiah was a better place to meet than All Souls Church. It was planned accordingly.[68]

Bellows wanted a convention for the transaction of business, not a mass meeting to encourage the brethren to make speeches. This was not the way the traditional Autumnal Conventions had operated, any more than it was the way the Free Religious Association at a later date would operate. That a genuine representative body, prepared to make responsible recommendations for the benefit of the whole denomination, was something new in Unitarian experience, Bellows was well aware. He therefore sought to do what planning could do to ensure that the convention would attend to its business. But he had a very clear sense of the difference between making sure that conclusions were reached in an orderly fashion, and making sure that certain desired conclusions were reached. "I feel the importance," he wrote to Hale, "of doing nothing by *mere force* of *machinery* which does not *legitimately belong* to machinery!"

> To carry a policy, force conclusions, or prevent serious & thotful debate is no plan of mine. Let us profoundly & conscientiously respect the spirit & antecedents of the Body in the regard we pay to the rights of minorities. I only want what is necessarily a part of arithmetic & mechanics, to go smoothly—so that the true spirit of the occasion may find easy grooves to slip in, & the heavenly steed, not jump off

the track, because the *human* harness breaks—all that honest arrangement can do, must be done beforehand.[69]

In view of the hours that had gone into detailed planning, Hale
could hardly keep a straight face when Gannett took him aside "to
express his surprise that we had not formed a precise programme of
operations!" But it was no intention of Hale's to tell him of it "a moment before it was announced on the housetops."[70] Mrs. Bellows, on
the other hand, knew only too well what was going on, and was exhausted by it (and by a severe case of hives): "I do not hesitate to say
to *you* of mature experience," she wrote to Bellows's sister, "that I entirely disapprove of the *high pressure* rate at which our dear Henry
always keeps himself & all who are willing subjects to this rushing &
driving system."[71]

III

The opening event of the convention was the service of worship in
Bellows's church on Tuesday evening, April 4. "The church was
crowded," Nannie Bellows wrote to her brother, "& Lizzie Kendall & I
went early to get seats. The singing was fine, & everything went off
well."[72] James Freeman Clarke's sermon argued that the time had
come for a new "change of base" for Christianity, so that it might include all those who are practically Christians in their daily lives but
who cannot accept what passes for orthodox Christianity. The spirit
of the sermon was inclusive, emphasizing that a wider cooperation is
possible when it is based on a concern for Christian action rather than
on doctrine. Like Bellows, Clarke sought a middle ground which was
neither "Creeds and Ceremonies" on the one side nor "Naturalism and
Deism" on the other, but which would enable both wings to unite and
to draw in others who were Liberal Christian in fact though not in
affiliation.[73] A careful reading of the sermon reveals passages where
Clarke picked up themes from Bellows's public and private exhorta-
tions; but it was his own sermon, and not Bellows's. "Father did not
think the sermon a very able one," Nannie Bellows reported, "but its
spirit was eminently Christian & conciliatory, & both the right & left
wing were pleased, & felt more amicably disposed towards each other
than before its delivery."[74]

The convention assembled for its first business session on Wednesday morning at the Broadway Atheneum, formerly Dr. Osgood's church. Governor Andrew of Massachusetts was elected president according to plan, and the Reverend E. E. Hale presented on behalf of the committee of arrangements a series of routine resolutions dealing with the organization of the work of the convention. At that point, A. A. Low of the Church of the Saviour in Brooklyn, for whom Clarke's sermon had been too conciliatory in tone, attempted to introduce a series of resolutions which would have established for the convention a creedal basis of a very conservative Christian kind. This unanticipated turn of events seemed to Bellows to be an attempt to split the convention. Though the conservative tone of the resolutions did not bother him, to introduce a creedal basis was "contrary to the pacific spirit, which it was so important to maintain in the convention."[75] By Bellows's immediate intervention, the resolutions were first ruled out of order and, when introduced again later, were laid on the table until the very end of the convention, when they were referred to the Council of the conference and never heard of again. "Never shall I forget," recalled John White Chadwick, after Bellows's death, "the noble scorn with which at the first meeting of the Conference he brought to naught the counsels of a clique that would have foisted on us a creed of desiccated phrases that had been secretly prepared by one of the most honored citizens of our own city."[76] Since Low was a wealthy man who carried great weight in the community, Bellows was fearful that no one else would call him to account if he did not, "& so he had to take the disagreeable business onto his own shoulders."[77]

For Bellows, the ground on which the convention should properly stand was not represented by Low's creedalism, but by two resolutions prepared by the Business Committee, and adopted at the beginning of the afternoon session of the first day. The first declared the obligation of the Unitarian body to organize on a more comprehensive plan, "but always on principles accordant with its Congregational or independent character." The second stated that decisions and resolutions should be understood as expressive of the opinion of the majority only,

> committing in no degree those who object to them, claiming no other than a moral authority over the members of the Convention, or the Churches represented here, and are all dependent wholly for their effect upon the consent they command on their own merits.

The subsequent actions of the convention were taken in the context of these affirmations, which were suggested in preliminary form in a letter from Bellows to Hale on March 28.[78]

The rest of Wednesday was devoted, as planned, to reports from the American Unitarian Association, the Western Conference, and other bodies concerned with the work of the denomination. The agenda was arranged deliberately so that the matter of permanent organization would come up on the second day. By this time, it was assumed, the convention would have discovered some sense of corporate identity, its members would have got accustomed to working together, and the laymen might have got over their initial inclination to let the ministers do all the talking.[79] In a general way, this is precisely what happened, though the laymen did not take as large a part in debate as Bellows had hoped. While certain of the radicals later accused Bellows of controlling the convention in dictatorial fashion, what came out of the deliberations was clearly an expression of the will of the delegates. Governor Andrew was certainly in control of the convention from a parliamentary point of view, and Bellows and Hale were on guard against any more maneuvers of the kind Low had attempted. One of them, they had agreed, would always be on the floor of the convention when the other had to be absent at a committee meeting. But if Bellows was a strong leader of the convention, as doubtless he was, he was a leader by the consent of his followers, and it was their objectives as much as his that were achieved.

Wednesday afternoon, a committee on permanent organization was authorized, consisting of twelve delegates, with Bellows as chairman. Since crucial recommendations came out of the deliberations of this committee, more particularly with respect to the name of the new organization and the preamble of the constitution, it is unfortunate that we have no record of its discussions. There is one bit of hearsay reported by Edward C. Towne which indicates that intransigence on the part of William G. Eliot of St. Louis was one reason for the conservative wording of the preamble.[80] What position Bellows took on the matter in committee is not known. Since the committee did not accept Bellows's suggestion with respect to the name of the organization—his clear preference was "The Liberal Christian Church of America"—it is plain that it did not meekly follow his bidding. In any event, in debate he loyally and vigorously supported the recommendations of his committee.

The draft constitution and bylaws were presented on Thursday morning. The constitution was a simple document, consisting of a preamble and eight articles. It envisaged a permanent organization, to be styled the "National Conference of Unitarian Churches," to meet annually, composed of three delegates (including the minister) from each church, a council to be responsible between annual sessions, and an advisory relationship with the A.U.A. and other denominational organs, which would continue to be "the instruments of its power."[81]

It soon became apparent that the only really controversial issue was the degree of inclusiveness the organization was to stand for. A year later, this issue was to be debated at Syracuse in terms of a proposed revision of the preamble, which included references to the "Lord Jesus Christ" and his "kingdom," which the radicals regarded as creedal in effect. At New York, however, the question came up rather in terms of the name of the organization. When James Freeman Clarke attempted to amend the name by adding the words "and Independent" after the word "Unitarian," his desire to broaden the scope of the organization was one with which Bellows sympathized. But Bellows was a realistic negotiator, and he may well have felt that the agreements reached in committee had best be adhered to, lest the whole uneasy relationship with conservatives like Eliot come unstuck.

The laity, as it seemed to Bellows, had brought a strong conservative tone to the meeting, which proved to be a limitation on the kind of consensus that was possible. *"We must not aim at the best,"* Bellows had written to Hale, *"but at what can be successfully carried."* He was prepared therefore to go no further than a broad consensus in the convention permitted. Even though he himself would have liked a more inclusive or broad-church position, he was not going to press an issue if there was a risk of stimulating "a disputatious, carping & personal spirit."[82] He therefore urged Clarke to withdraw his amendment, with the understanding that the whole broad-church issue would be reexamined at the next annual session. After a number of modifications of the name were proposed without any of them gaining wide support, the article was adopted with but one dissenting vote.

The remaining articles as reported by the committee of twelve were accepted unanimously. A ninth article was then proposed by the Reverend Charles G. Ames of Albany in order to state explicitly that there was no intention of excluding any church that desired to cooperate for Christian work. Once again, the intent of the proposal was one with which Bellows was in agreement, but he feared that to press the matter, given the temper of the convention, would be to "swamp the boat." Since no acceptable wording could be worked out on the floor of the convention, the motion was finally laid on the table, even though it clearly had strong support. Final adoption of the constitution was by an overwhelming vote, perhaps as much as ten to one.[83]

Throughout the proceedings, Bellows sought consistently to prevent either the conservatives or the radicals from forcing an issue that would split the convention. Once an accommodation had been reached in the committee of twelve, Bellows stuck with the agreement, even on points with which he was not wholly content. The threat from A. A. Low and his conservative group was handled relatively easily, because its creedalism was unpalatable to most Unitarians, Christians and radicals alike. The problem of the radicals was more difficult, because they insisted that creedalism lurked in Christian terminology, even when anticreedal Christians like Bellows protested that there was no intention of using the preamble as a creedal test. Bellows's sense of frustration in trying to communicate with the radicals was such that towards the end of the convention he did lapse into language which he afterwards regretted and for which he apologized, but which the radicals never allowed to be forgotten. He objected, he said, to bodies of men who claimed to be the "peculiar champions of liberty."

> He yielded to no one in devotion to the spirit of liberty. If intolerance was to be found at all, it was among those who sneered at conservatives and thanked God that they were not such—sneered at those who wanted to conserve that which they deemed eternal truth. He belonged to that class who wanted to control the spirit of the age. He accepted none of the taunts about the disgrace of this convention. He desired the sympathy and affection of both sides, but if he had to choose between the two he frankly avowed that he would go rather with Orthodoxy in any form in which it could be stated than with those who would put Jesus Christ into comparative contempt. We have made a constitution for the purpose of holding the latter to it, and if the issue is made we shall gain ten firm, good Christians for every one we lose.[84]

IV

Bellows was well pleased with the outcome of the convention. About six hundred lay and ministerial delegates had attended, representing well over three quarters of the churches. Not half a dozen ministers of importance had stayed away: "Dr. Furness, Putnam, Weiss, the two Ellises & Chandler Robbins were the only absentees of any note." The process of organization had been accomplished in a way that represented the desires of the majority, "on a conservative *preamble,* but with full independence in the individual churches." Bellows was especially pleased to discover that neither wing of the denomination was as large as some had supposed: "The Unitarian Denomination, which we had been talking of as if it were like a night-hawk all wings, turned out to be *an ostrich,* all body, with very insignificant wings, either right or left." The weakness of the radicals was a surprising development; and Bellows concluded, somewhat prematurely, that the denomination had "finished up *Naturalism* & Transcendentalism & Parkerism." In short, the convention "was an *absolute & entire success.*"[85]

Bellows's satisfaction at what was accomplished, even if it fell short of his larger hopes, was widely shared throughout the denomination; but there was one conspicuous dissenting voice. Octavius Brooks Frothingham had gone to the convention reluctantly, predisposed to be disappointed. Predictably, he found what he sought. On the following Sunday, which was Palm Sunday, he preached on "The Unitarian Convention and the Times." He accused the convention of turning away from the proclaimed goal of the Liberal Church of America to a narrower sectarianism than ever before. "The Liberal Body shrunk from its own principle, and disowned the purport of its own summons." Bellows himself came in for specific attack: the convention "clapped its hands when intellectual radicalism was denounced and spurned in intemperate language by the leading spirit of the Convention." Like Christ deserted by the multitude immediately following the hosannas of Palm Sunday, the liberal principle was deserted at the close of the convention. "There has never been a Convention so narrow and blind and stubborn as it was."[86]

Frothingham's sermon was soon printed in the *Friend of Progress,* the editor of which had his own comment on the convention. It was "a sad and humiliating disappointment. . . ." Clarke's sermon was "inconsistent in substance, incoherent in arrangement, irresolute in purpose, and wild in aim." The words of the radicals had been "few, simple, calm, and sweet"; the words of their opponents were "many, forced, violent, and bitter." In sum, the convention

> added more sectarianism to that which already existed; it disavowed the radicalism which its letter of invitation made boast of; it repelled the men who were more competent than any others, perhaps, to do the work it proposed and marked out; it drew the liberal body back within the limits of a local denomination, and rebaptized it with an old name suggestive of dogmatism and saturated with controversial animus; and instead of the great liberal church of America, it gave us an enlarged and stereotyped edition of the American Unitarian Association.[87]

Other radical criticism of the convention was much more temperate, and helps to explain why it was that most of the radicals remained within the fold. Some of the most acute comments, perhaps, were made by Francis Ellingwood Abbot, who eventually did abandon the denomination, but whose disaffection is to be dated from the Syracuse meeting of the National Conference the fall of the following year. Abbot reported on the New York convention to his church in Dover, N.H., in a sermon revised for the *Christian Register*. The spirit of the convention, he stated, was "in a very marked degree, harmonious, decorous, and conciliatory"; remarks which were not of that character were "made the most of by the reporters." The formal basis of the new National Conference, as represented by the preamble and the use of the Unitarian name, represented a sectarian retreat from the broad vision of the Liberal Church of America which, according to Abbot, had "saddened and disappointed" many people.

He himself was hopeful, however, for he found the "principles which practically guided the action of this convention" to have been better than the sectarian name and the conservative preamble it adopted. Ultimately, those principles would prevail. The retention of the name Unitarian "was simply the result of old associations"; what really mattered was that the convention voted down by large majorities "all attempts to affix a dogmatic or theological meaning" to it. The sentiment of the convention was "unmistakably opposed to creeds of any form," and so he regarded those of his fellow radicals "who interpret the preamble as a creed, as decidedly in the wrong. . . ." His objection to the preamble was not that it was a creed, but that it had the ambiguity or equivocation of a verbal compromise, when with more attention and discussion a better preamble that more faithfully represented the common ground of unity could have been worked out and adopted. "I am full of hope," he insisted, "and not one whit discouraged by the purely embryonic results of our first great conference." The first steps had been taken, and the logic of freedom implicit in the actions of the convention itself would make for better results another time.[88]

It was Abbot's failure to persuade the Conference to improve its faulty handiwork at the next meeting, at Syracuse in 1866, that led to his break with the denomination. Two things had happened meanwhile. One of them was that Abbot himself had encountered serious discontent and criticism in his own parish in Dover, a circumstance which may well have fostered a more uncompromising spirit on his part. The other was that the majority at Syracuse seems to have been persuaded that it was better to stick with the preamble as already adopted, since there was no assurance that any other wording would be any more widely acceptable. Both Dr. Clarke and Dr. Osgood acknowledged that Abbot's substitute wording, as proposed in 1866, might well have been adopted the year before had it been presented then; but to eliminate Christian terminology already approved would seem, rightly or wrongly, to be an abandonment of the Christian tradition. At that point, the Free Religious Association was conceived.[89]

One other radical response to the New York convention must be mentioned. It was the pamphlet entitled *Unitarian Fellowship and Liberty,* by Edward C. Towne, minister of the Medford church and a close associate of Frothingham. It was a bitter attack on the convention and the part Bellows played in it. It accused him of having assumed the role of dictator, and of making his own theological opinions the test of Christian communion. The preamble was interpreted as a creedal statement deliberately phrased by Bellows and the committee of twelve in order to drive out the radicals. At one point in the course of the debate, Thomas D. Eliot, the brother of William G. Eliot and a layman from New Bedford, proposed a restriction on the length of speeches, and the convention assented. Towne believed that this was a parliamentary device resorted to by "the managers on the platform" to prevent the radicals from having their say, and that Eliot "was their mouthpiece." These charges cannot be supported by any evidence thus far uncovered, and they are not easily reconciled with what we do know of the plans and intentions of "the managers on the platform."[90]

A curious aspect of the publication of Towne's pamphlet is that it is dated April 27, 1866, more than a year after the events with which it deals. It does not seem to represent Towne's initial reaction. As late as December 1865, Joseph Henry Allen wrote to Bellows: "I hope you observed the prompt & handsome way in which Towne settled the case of the man who 'spat' on you in the Commonwealth."[91] One cannot help wondering what happened to sour Towne and whether a sequence of events in the fall of 1865 may be the explanation. Towne submitted an article somewhat critical of Frederic Henry Hedge for publication in the *Christian Examiner,* of which Allen was then editor. Since Bellows was to assume direction of the magazine at the beginning of 1866, Allen solicited his opinion. Bellows replied that he wanted all shades of Unitarian opinion represented in the journal. He did regret that this particular article was scheduled for publication in the first issue for which he would be regarded as responsible; but he said he would not decline it, "as it is earnest, well-studied & presents legitimate considerations—which so far as they are wrong & untenable need to be met—& cannot be met until they are proposed in this public way."[92] Allen suggested to Towne that publication be deferred to the next following issue. But early in January, long after the article had gone to the printer, Towne withdrew it, despite Allen's remonstrances, on the grounds that its publication would put Bellows in a wrong position.[93] It is plausible to argue that Towne resented Allen's handling of the matter, and exploded in all directions against the way in which Bellows was emerging as the dominant figure in the denomination.[94]

V

Because of the strong tradition of intellectual freedom among Unitarians, the radical attack on Bellows has often been applauded. Yet the fact remains that it was Bellows, not the radicals, who realized the necessity of coming to grips with the implications for social organization posed by the development of industrial society after the Civil War. It was Bellows who made Unitarians recognize that they would have to reconstruct outmoded forms of organization if they were to survive.

It was Bellows, not the radicals, who attempted a reaffirmation of the tradition of intellectual liberty within the framework of inescapable institutional development. Bellows, the theological "conservative," was the most important institutional innovator of that generation of Unitarians.

It was Bellows, too, who provided leadership for the mediating group within the Unitarian body, and thereby kept the denomination from plunging into a fatal schism. Because no division took place, it is all too easy to assume that no such danger existed. Yet the fear of division was demonstrably real, whether the threat was real or not. "Is there a serious movement to divide the denomination into 'Evangelical and Radical'?" A. D. Mayo inquired of Hale.[95] A. P. Peabody, Chandler Robbins, Gannett, Sears, and the Ellises were all thought by supporters of the convention to prefer a division; and there was a genuine feeling of relief when the outcome seemed to indicate that that danger had been averted. "It seems to me that the great gain of the meeting is that it decides the future of the Unitarian body," wrote W. W. Newell. "It is clear that we are to have no division. . . . Holding fast to this basis, if there is to be any change in old style Unitarianism it will be gradual, not sudden and convulsing."[96] Bellows's success in constructing a broad middle-ground consensus has to be weighed against his failure to satisfy the scruples of Octavius Brooks Frothingham.

For services such as these, there were not wanting men of his own generation to give him the praise that was his due. Hedge called him "our Bishop, our Metropolitan," exercising his functions "by universal consent of the brethren."[97] John White Chadwick, himself a radical, declared that "almost every best thing that has been devised for the last seventeen years within the limits of the Unitarian denomination has taken its initiative from him or to his splendid advocacy owed its practical success."[98] And Bartol said, quite simply: "Dr. Bellows is the only leader the Unitarian body has ever had."[99]

FROM STANDING ORDER
TO SECULARISM

I

In general, it may be argued, dominant majorities in any society will be insensitive as to the feelings of disadvantaged minorities, and will find it difficult to understand what the minorities are complaining about. Specifically, dominant religious groups will be far less sensitive than religious minorities to situations in which religious freedom is abridged. A given practice, such as prayer or Bible reading in the public schools, may seem wholly unexceptionable to the majority, who may well feel that no real issue of separation of church and state is involved. Minorities who feel coerced, however, will be quick to argue that basic issues of principle are at stake. Hence it is possible to have agreement on the abstract principle of separation of church and state, and still have bitter conflict over the applicability of this principle to particular situations.

This distinction between the attitude of dominant majorities on the one hand and disadvantaged minorities on the other has a very particular relevance for the history of Unitarian and Universalist attitudes towards church-state relationships. The New England Unitarians came out of the Standing Order, while the Universalists were in revolt against it. The merged denomination has a heritage, therefore, which begins with a dual perspective, one of them that of the "establishment"—a word here bearing a double freightage of meaning—and the other that of the disadvantaged or "alienated" groups in society.

The term "Standing Order" is the traditional one used to designate the special relationship between church and state in the Puritan colonies of New England. These institutional arrangements were not finally abolished until 1818 in Connecticut, 1819 in New Hampshire, and 1833 in Massachusetts. They required the local towns and parishes to provide for the support of public worship, by taxation if the inhabitants failed to make proper provision for such support by voluntary contributions. What this meant in practice was that, in most New England towns, the costs of building and maintaining the meeting house, and the salary of the minister, were paid by local assessments on the inhabitants. Exemptions were granted, however, beginning in the 1720s for members of recognized minority groups, such as the Baptists, so that their money would go to the support of their own worship.

These arrangements were accepted without qualm by the first generation of New England Unitarians, and were defended by them as being neither an infringement of liberty of conscience, nor a violation of the principle of separation of church and state. Since we automatically reject the position our forebears took on these matters, we need to try to understand the logic by which they defended the institutions with which they were familiar.[1] Perhaps the best place to begin is with their basic assumption that tax support of public worship is to be justified, not as a benefit to religion or the church, but as a benefit to society. The coercive powers of the state, they argued, can restrain men from committing crime, but they cannot make men positively virtuous. Yet no society can function unless its members are, for the most part, persons of integrity and public concern, who share a set of moral values making for good citizenship. Society, for its own survival, must encourage men who accept as their responsibility the elevation and transmission of the moral values on which civilized existence itself depends.

Our ancestors therefore turned to the ministers of the churches, and called upon them to perform the public function of clarifying and sustaining the moral tone of the community. This civic role of the minister is nicely indicated by the refusal of the drafters of the Massachusetts Constitution of 1780 to use the term "minister," replacing it with the phrase: "public . . . teachers of piety, religion and morality." The civic function of the "public teacher" in his relationship with the town or parish was clearly differentiated, in theory at least, from his ecclesiastical function as minister of the church, which was a voluntary association of believers within the community but not coterminous with it. With the internal concerns of the churches, the state scrupulously did not interfere, because church and state, it was agreed, must be kept separate. But to ask a minister to serve also as a "public teacher" of morality was regarded as no more a violation of the principle of separation of church and state than for us to rely largely on ministers, priests, and rabbis to act as agents of the state in the solemnization of marriages. But the state could hardly require ministers to serve also as "public teachers" without making certain that they were properly recompensed for their public services; hence the provision for their support, by taxation if necessary.

When the Standing Order in New England came under attack in the latter part of the eighteenth century, it was this rationale for it that was set forth with increasing explicitness and clarity. And since it was within the churches of the Standing Order that Unitarianism was developing, some of the most explicit statements of it are to be found in the writings of the theological liberals of the day. Thus we find Channing defending the Standing Order in 1820, in a sermon entitled "Religion a Social Principle." The sermon was occasioned by the debates then in progress in the convention meeting in Boston to recommend amendments to the Constitution of the Commonwealth. The Christian religion, Chann   inted out to the delegates, is "singularly important to *free* commun.   Religion "diminishes the necessity of publick restraints"; by its "purifying and restraining influence" operating on men's hearts, it diminishes the necessity for a powerful government which would be a threat to their liberties. It follows that it is not only within the power but should be the policy of government to support Christianity as tending "powerfully to publick order and happiness. . . ." To those who declared that this matter can safely be left by the state to the voluntary action of individuals, he replied: "But it is not wise for a community to leave to private discretion any great interest, in which its safety is involved."[2]

These presuppositions, so axiomatic to supporters of the Standing Order, and not least to theological liberals, were far from obvious to certain minority groups. The Baptists, under the leadership of Isaac Backus, were especially forceful in arguing that what seemed to the dominant majority a fair and equal arrangement was actually not equal at all; and they questioned pointedly the assumption that religion would not flourish on a basis of voluntary support. The law provided that persons who belonged to minority or "dissenting" religious groups could have their money go to the support of their own worship. But a long history of litigation had already proved how hard it was for minority groups to gain the recognition that entitled them to tax relief. The equality that was theoretically granted by the Constitution was actually dependent on the action of local petty officials, whose lack of sympathy with minorities tempted them into various forms of harassment. But even had there been no problem of this kind, the necessity to secure a specific exemption from the regular parish rates seemed to the minority sects to be basically invidious.

The Baptists were not the only ones who learned that equality was not equal when the terms of equality were set by the majority. The Universalists whom John Murray gathered into a congregation in Gloucester in 1779 made the same discovery. Having organized themselves as an "independent church," having designated Murray to be their minister, and having constructed at their own expense a building for worship, they assumed that they were relieved, under the provisions of the new Constitution, from further obligation to support the minister of the parish. But the parish authorities continued to assess them on the grounds that there had been no official withdrawal from the parish, and that their so-called "independent church" had not been organized in such a way that it could be recognized in law as a distinct "religious sect or denomination" whose members were entitled to exemption. On the first score, their withdrawal had been without formality or explanation, and all attempts to learn what the grievances might be had been met with "silent contempt." On the second point, the parish argued "that as they have never been incorporated by any order or authority known in this commonwealth, nor at any time laid before us as a parish any reasons why they should be exempted, we cannot levy a lawful tax without including them."[3]

An even more basic issue was involved, in which the differences between the perspectives of a majority and those of a minority come into especially sharp focus. The supporters of the Standing Order argued with a good deal of persuasiveness that a civilized social order depended on a set of moral values held in common by the people. For them, axiomatically, this meant moral values grounded in religion. Equally axiomatically, as Channing's writings are enough to demonstrate, this meant Christianity. Furthermore, as the wording of the Massachusetts Constitution indicates, it meant Protestant Christianity.

The Universalists discovered that it meant only certain kinds of Protestant Christianity. The law provided that a minority group might be exempt from parish taxes if its members supported their own public teacher of piety, religion, and morality. But John Murray obviously could not be regarded as such a teacher because he preached a doctrine of universal salvation which undercut the accepted sanctions of morality. As the spokesmen for the First Parish put it: "Can a man, who publickly discards the doctrine of God's moral government—of future rewards and punishments—urge, with a good face, or with any hope of success, the practice of morality? Can he, consistently, preach up morality, when he at the same time saps its very foundation . . . ?"[4]

With some reluctance, the Universalists of Gloucester finally conformed to the standards of the majority on procedural matters. They secured incorporation from the legislature, and they reordained Murray in a ceremony that none could mistake. The question whether he might be regarded as a teacher of morality was eventually decided in his favor in the courts, even though the Universalists argued against the propriety of settling matters of doctrine by litigation: "if the courts of law in this State are to go into an inquiry of this kind, the conscience of the judges will be the standard of religious sentiment, and the only inquiry upon matters of faith will be, What was the opinion of the court in the last trial?"[5]

The Universalists and other religious minorities had a strong sense of oppression, with which we easily sympathize. Yet the supporters of the Standing Order had no consciousness of being oppressors. On the contrary, in numerous instances they can be found attempting to accommodate their concern for public order and safety to the sensitivities of the religious minorities. What ultimately happened was that the Standing Order became so riddled with exemptions and exceptions, introduced to meet the objections of minorities, that it was no longer functional. Then even its onetime supporters were ready to abandon it. The end in Massachusetts came with so little opposition that it can hardly be represented as a triumph of principle over self-interest. It was a pragmatic, and doubtless overdue, recognition of the fact that a social institution that could be plausibly defended in an essentially homogeneous society made no sense in a pluralistic one.

A few Unitarians there were who argued in favor of the Standing Order to the end.[6] But a more realistic note was struck by the editors of the *Christian Examiner*. This is a question, they declared, "which must be decided with a constant reference to existing circumstances and the state of public opinion." Is it worthwhile, they went on to ask, "to contend very earnestly for the theoretical and express recognition of a power in the hands of government, which the government does not exert, and which there is not the smallest probability it ever will exert? . . . And as for the prescriptive rights and immunities of the old, or territorial parishes, is it not clear that, by the multiplication of legal evasions, they are, practically speaking, already reduced to a nullity?"[7] The Standing Order was already in shambles, and it remained only to clear away the debris.

II

Even though the Unitarians acquiesced in the dissolution of the Standing Order, for which they had been among the leading spokesmen, they continued to assume that it was they who represented the interests of society as a whole, as opposed to minority and sectarian religious groups. It is, after all, easy for dominant majorities to suppose that it is their particular set of values that prevents civilization from declining into barbarism and superstition. The liberals were actually now a small minority themselves; but they were shielded for the time being from the implications of that fact by virtue of their continued control of many positions of decision-making in the community. The time was coming, faster than they realized, when the Episcopalians would supplant them. But for a long time—and, indeed, has the habit wholly died out?—they spoke out vigorously against the narrow sectarian spirit of all other groups, a spirit from which they themselves were happily free.[8]

They were also reluctant to abandon the basic rationale by which the Standing Order had been justified. That rationale was that civil society must depend much more on the positive virtue of its citizens than on negative restraint and punishment; and so the state in its own interest must sustain and encourage all those agencies of the mind and spirit that nurture morality. The function must still be performed, they seem to be saying, even if other instrumentalities must be found to perform it. And so the liberals turned to the common schools, and gave enthusiastic support to the leadership of Horace Mann, himself a Unitarian, in the policy of promoting what he understood to be nonsectarian moral education in the schools. It is surely no mere coincidence that the movement for free public education gained momentum in Massachusetts as the Standing Order was disintegrating. As Channing put it, in 1833: "We know not how society can be aided more than by the formation of a body of wise and efficient educators. We know not any class which would contribute so much to the stability of the state, and to domestic happiness. Much as we respect the ministry of the gospel, we believe that it must yield in importance to the office of training the young."[9]

Horace Mann became the first secretary of the Massachusetts Board of Education in 1837. The policy he was to follow, and which he made very much his own, had already been laid down by the legislature. In 1827, a law was enacted that began by enjoining instruction in "the principles of piety, justice, and sacred regard to truth," as "the basis upon which the Republican Constitution is founded," and ended by forbidding the use in schools of books "which are calculated to favor any particular religious sect or tenet."[10] On taking office, Mann quickly discovered that unobjectionable books of moral instruction were not easy to find, but he did not despair. In 1840, he restated the policy thus: "Although it may not be easy theoretically, to draw the line between those views of religious truth and of christian faith, which are common to all, and may, therefore, with propriety be inculcated in school, and those which, being peculiar to individual sects, are therefore by law excluded; still it is believed, that no practical difficulty occurs in the conduct of our schools in this respect."[11] In short, Mann was not an advocate of the elimination of religious training from the public schools, but rather wanted the inclusion of as much religion as the religious pluralism of society would permit. In this, his stand seems to have been no different from that of other Unitarians of that generation.

Mann soon discovered that he had underestimated the practical difficulties of implementing a policy of religion without sectarianism. The law of 1827 had been acceptable to orthodox congregationalists as well as Unitarian congregationalists; but it quickly became clear that there was disagreement as to what "nonsectarian" really meant. Mann was promptly embroiled in controversy with Frederick A. Packard, the secretary of the American Sunday School Union, who sought to introduce books of an evangelical religious nature into school libraries. Packard spoke for those for whom moral instruction as the basis of citizenship necessarily implied evangelical Protestantism, of a broadly nondenominational kind. Mann responded to such pressures by advocating the reading of the Bible, without commentary. While different sects might draw different doctrinal conclusions from the Bible, he argued, the sacred text was common to all.

The only trouble with Mann's solution to the problem was that it was a characteristically Unitarian one, which seemed to the orthodox to be as sectarian in actual fact as their proposals did to him. Behind it was the theological reductionism the liberals had inherited from eighteenth-century rationalism, as well as the biblicism that had been their chief reliance in the period of the Unitarian controversy. The bland assumption of the Unitarians that only they could be trusted to avoid sectarianism did not improve the atmosphere in which the discussion was carried on. And if the complaints from the Orthodox were not enough, before long the Catholics were complaining that the reading of the Bible without commentary was a typically underhanded Protestant way of attacking their faith, since the version used was the King James translation, and the avoidance of commentary was an expression of the Protestant dogma of private judgment.[12] It would appear that there was no way to draw the line between the nonsectarian moral and religious values that undergird civil society and the sectarian concerns of particular groups which would not plausibly seem to be in itself an expression of sectarianism by one group or another.

In New York a similar clash of opinion developed in 1840–42 over the use of state funds to support the work of the Public School Society of that city. In the absence of a system of publicly controlled common schools, a considerable proportion of the children of the city were enrolled in schools organized by a privately sponsored society. While the officers of the Public School Society insisted that their schools were nonsectarian, the Catholics protested that they were actually thoroughly Protestant, if not anti-Catholic, in tone. Governor Seward, sympathetic to these protests, and doubtless not unmindful of the political implications of his stand, recommended that the Catholics also receive state support for their own schools, so that their children might "be instructed by teachers speaking the same language with themselves and professing the same faith." After all, while these might be the children of foreigners, they were themselves citizens who should not be deprived of the opportunity of qualifying "for the high responsibilities of citizenship."[13]

The Catholics applauded, while the Protestant majority, convinced that schools under Catholic auspices would not make good Americans out of the children of foreigners, protested vigorously. The final result was the establishment of a public Board of Education, the promulgation of explicit restrictions on sectarian religious instruction in the schools, and the ultimate demise of the Public School Society. Since the schools established by the Society were absorbed into the new system, a Protestant atmosphere did not disappear at once, but the schools did eventually become more responsive to their immediate constituency. Bishop Hughes and the Catholics would have been delighted to receive public funds for schools that they themselves sponsored, but they decidedly preferred no religious indoctrination at all to the nonsectarian Protestantism that had prevailed. As Hughes put it: "If the children are to be educated promiscuously, let religion in every shape and form be excluded. Let not the Protestant version of the Scriptures, Protestant forms of prayers, Protestant hymns, be forced on the children of Catholics, Jews, and others, as at present, in the schools for the support of which their parents pay taxes as well as Presbyterians."[14] Of course, the time was to come when Unitarians, conscious of their own minority status, would be converted to the logic of Hughes's position.

After the Civil War, the question of the use of the Bible in the public schools continued to be agitated, a persistent element in the discussion being the Roman Catholic threat to American democracy. A controversy in Cincinnati in 1869–72 occasioned much discussion among Unitarians and Universalists, and revealed an extremely interesting pattern of responses. In September 1869, a proposal was made whereby the Catholic parochial schools would be taken over by the public School Board and operated in all respects according to its rules. The Catholics would use the facilities on Saturdays and Sundays; but on regular school days all religious instruction would be prohibited, "including all religious books, music, and the Bible." Instead of seeing this as opening the way to the secularization of Catholic education, the Protestants regarded it as infiltration of Catholic education into the public schools. Although the plan was soon dropped, the suggested ban on religious instruction came before the Board for independent consideration, and was finally passed. The issue was then taken to the courts, and an injunction was issued preventing the Board from implementing the new policy. On appeal, the Supreme Court of the State of Ohio reversed the decision on the grounds that this was properly a matter for legislative discretion.[15]

Two Unitarians were members of the School Board, and their involvement insured that the issues would be discussed widely in Unitarian and Universalist periodicals. Amory D. Mayo was minister of the Church of the Redeemer and a leader of Christian Unitarianism in the West; he had originally been a Universalist and still contributed to the *Universalist Quarterly*. Thomas Vickers, the other Unitarian on the Board, was in his first pastorate at the First Congregational Unitarian Church. This church had something of a radical tradition, since Vickers's two immediate predecessors had been Sidney H. Morse and Moncure D. Conway. Vickers himself was identified with the Free Religious Association, and publications like the *Index,* edited by Francis Ellingwood Abbot, were vigorous in their support of him.[16]

It is tempting to regard Mayo and Vickers as symbols of two rival positions in the Unitarian denomination, and to assume a simple correlation between their views on the school issue and their theological stances. The picture, however, is more complicated than that. For if Unitarianism in those days had two wings, it also had a body—like an ostrich, Henry W. Bellows insisted, "with a very heavy Body & very small wings."[17] If Mayo and Vickers spoke for the two wings, it was a committee under the chairmanship of the Rev. James De Normandie, reporting to the National Conference in 1872, which spoke for the body. And there is even a fourth position, which begins to emerge in somewhat tentative form in an unsigned article entitled "The National Church," which was printed in the magazine *Old and New* in 1870.

Mayo's position was a continuation of the tradition for which Horace Mann had been spokesman. It was that the schools had an obligation to instruct children in the principles of religion, while carefully avoiding sectarian indoctrination, and that the Bible was a proper instrument for such instruction. As he stated it: "religion and morality . . . are the very foundation of human society itself, the basement structure of their whole form of government, the sanction of all their laws, and the final judge of all their public policy."[18] He saw himself as contending against two enemies of the public schools, the Catholics and the secularists. The Catholics he accused of sectarianism for their failure to acknowledge that the use of the Bible was nonsectarian; their ultimate goal, he believed, was "the utter destruction of our American system of common schools. . . ." The secularists, on the other hand, were led chiefly by "foreign exiles, cast upon our shores by European revolutions, aided by a small circle of native speculators in politics and religion." Their program was to subvert the traditional American political philosophy, and to set men adrift on a sea of Atheism, "with no eternal landmarks or obligations."[19]

Vickers was indeed a secularist on these matters. Speaking before the Free Religious Association in May 1870, he denied that God or Christ had anything to do with the government of the United States, or that the American government was in any sense founded on the Christian religion. The true ends of the state, he was reported as having said, "had nothing to do with the propagation or even the recognition of religion. He would insist on the absolute secularization of the State."[20] While information on Vickers is scanty, one senses that he found the Protestant Christian flavor of the public schools offensive, just as the Catholics did.

At first glance, the report of De Normandie's committee to the National Conference in 1872 may seem to be simply a compromise, since it begins with Mayo's presuppositions but ends with Vickers's practical recommendations. Actually it has an integrity of its own, in which pragmatic considerations loom large. The committee had been established by vote of the Conference in 1870, in response to the Cincinnati debate. It included both conservatives like Mayo (who was, however, unable to participate in its deliberations) and free religionists like John White Chadwick. It would appear to have been a good, representative committee. The report reasserted the religious presuppositions of American education; it insisted that the public school system exists to fit all citizens for the best possible citizenship; and it rejected Romanism as hostile to democracy. But it declared that Bible reading in the schools was performing no genuine educational function, but was reduced to being a symbol of Protestant domination: "the Bible, as introduced and now read in our schools, is merely the banner and battle-cry of Protestantism and a sectarian service." The committee therefore offered a series of resolutions based on the principle that a symbol of sectarian Protestantism should be eliminated as a barrier to the inclusion of minority groups in the schools. Chadwick would have liked to have had the Conference recommend the "exclusion" of Bible reading; the majority preferred a slightly less provocative wording: "we nevertheless would not insist upon it as an essential or useful part of our public school system."[21]

The fourth position is somewhat more elusive, and not only so because the clearest expression of it is in an unsigned essay. It identifies the theological position of liberal Christianity with the philosophical presuppositions of American democracy. Religious liberalism then becomes what has more recently been termed "America's real religion," as contrasted both with Roman Catholicism and with evangelical Protestantism. Unitarianism and Universalism turn out to be the quintessential expression of American religious idealism, and an institutional form of the "National Church of America," which truly exists whether it has any complete institutional form or not. The National Church is "that method of Religious life, or opinion, which, in practice, determines the action or endeavor of the Nation." It may express itself through many instrumentalities, including church and state; and it is a matter of convenience or practical judgment in a given case what instrumentality is to be used. The only distinction between the provinces of church and state is "such as convenience orders from day to day. Education, charity, worship, are left to both, or to neither."[22] While the argument is not carried to the point of a specific application to the question of Bible reading, it suggests a pragmatic approach, just as De Normandie's report to the National Conference did.

The fact that the Cincinnati controversy produced a variety of responses suggests that the Unitarians and Universalists were moving into a new situation, in which familiar assumptions no longer sufficed. The conservative position taken by Mayo, to be sure, still sounds like the attempt of a dominant majority to reeducate and civilize peculiar un-American minorities, so that they might safely be admitted as responsible citizens.[23] But the other three positions are sensitive, though in different ways, to the question of what it means to be a minority group. This is doubtless clearest in the case of the radicals, whose theology itself made them suspect in the eyes of the Unitarian majority, and whose secularism made them feel persecuted by Christians generally. But the main body of Unitarians as well, represented by the National Conference, was learning that, whatever may once have been the case in eastern Massachusetts, in the country at large they were a small minority confronting in the public schools an all-pervasive ethos which they found as uncongenial as the Catholics did. As for the fourth position, the essay on the National Church may be read as an example of the way in which a small group compensates for its lack of numbers by making an extreme claim for its significance. There may not be many Unitarians, and of course there should be more; but numbers are not the important thing, since most Americans are really Unitarians without knowing it!

III

By the end of the century, something of a consensus seems to have been achieved. In 1901, the American Unitarian Association voted to establish a committee to study "the condition and progress of unsectarian education in American schools."[24] A preliminary report was submitted the following year by the chairman, Joseph Henry Crooker, who then elaborated the findings into a book published by the Association, entitled *Religious Freedom in American Education* (1903).

The minority consciousness that produced the committee and its report is quite explicit in the original vote and in the preliminary report, though it is carefully eliminated in the final book. The problem was that Unitarian parents could not find preparatory schools to which they might send their children without running the risk that the purity of their liberal religious faith might be contaminated. They have had to send them "to secondary schools where religious doctrines antagonistic to the Unitarian faith have been urgently taught or powerfully exemplified." The result has been that "hundreds of young people have been alienated from our faith and lost from our church." The committee therefore gave its support to schools like Hackley and Prospect Hill, under Unitarian auspices, where the religious atmosphere was "positive" but "theological neutrality" was secured.[25]

Crooker's book reported with approval that there were strong forces elsewhere in American education moving in the same direction. The modern state, and specifically the American state, he declared, is the secular state, which must therefore be supported by secular education: "The secularization of the State involves and necessitates the secularization of its schools." But a secular state must be theologically neutral, so it must "ignore" the protests of the churchman who objects "that it is unjust to tax him to support what he cannot use." By this claim, the churchman "puts himself above the authority of the State, which in matters pertaining to citizenship must be supreme." This does not mean, according to Crooker, that the public schools will be godless or unconcerned with moral values; rather they will be the instrumentalities by which the values of democratic citizenship—what some scholars have recently called "civic religion"—are communicated: "If there is any place which is really and pre-eminently godly, it is the Public School, where children of all sects, races, and conditions, meet upon absolute equality to acquire knowledge, to be trained in justice, fidelity, and universal fellowship, and to be inducted into the rights and sanctities of citizenship."[26]

Here we find Mayo's concern for the religious foundations of society married to Vickers's secularism, and the minority insistence on the banishment of offensive sectarian theology paving the way for the introduction of the theology of the National Church. The combination was so effective that Unitarians, whose thinking on problems of church and state had been in a constant process of development for two generations, were relieved of the necessity of altering their opinions on the matter for the next two.

NOTES

Chapter I: Rational Religion in Eighteenth-Century America:
Pages 1–21

1. W. W. Sweet, *Religion in the Development of American Culture* (New York, 1952), pp. 91–92.

2. George M. Stephenson, *The Puritan Heritage* (New York, 1952), pp. 86, 91.

3. Clifton E. Olmstead, *History of Religion in the United States* (Englewood Cliffs, N.J., 1960), pp. 155–191, 218–221.

4. W. G. Muelder and L. Sears, *The Development of American Philosophy* (Boston, c. 1940), pp. 65–110.

5. W. H. Werkmeister, *A History of Philosophical Ideas in America* (New York, c. 1949), pp. 18, 31–37. The one recent book that not only gives a decent balance between rationalism and evangelical religion but also shows an awareness that Deism was not the only kind of rational religion is Volume I of H. S. Smith, R. T. Handy, and L. A. Loetscher, *American Christianity* (New York, c. 1960); this book was not available when this lecture was originally prepared. But the traditional emphasis reappears in Winthrop S. Hudson, *Religion in America* (New York, c. 1965), in which the Great Awakening is given twenty-three pages, and rationalism less than three.

6. I. Woodbridge Riley, *American Philosophy, the Early Schools* (New York, 1907).

7. G. Adolf Koch, *Republican Religion* (New York, 1933); paperback edition issued in 1968 with the title *Religion of the American Enlightenment*.

8. A. C. McGiffert, *Protestant Thought before Kant* (New York, 1912), p. 189.

9. John H. Randall, Jr., *The Making of the Modern Mind* (Boston, 1926), p. 285.

10. Within the precincts of the Union Theological Seminary, an inverted form, "rational supernaturalism," is preferred. But this is just as infelicitous, and has even less to commend it than the original McGiffert-Randall concoction. The difficulty with "Supernatural Rationalism," after all, is not with the noun, but with the modifying adjective. "Rationalism" stands over against "evangelicalism" or "evangelical orthodoxy"; together they encompass much of eighteenth-century religion. But "supernaturalism" performs no such differentiating function in the

context of that century. An unsatisfactory adjective becomes even less satisfactory when made a substantive.

11. C. K. Shipton, *Sibley's Harvard Graduates*, Vol. IV (Cambridge, 1933), pp. 42–54.

12. "Appendix" to John Barnard, *A Proof of Jesus Christ His Being the Ancient Promised Messiah* (Boston, 1756).

13. Shipton, *Sibley*, Vol. V (Boston, 1937), pp. 265–278.

14. Edward Holyoke, *The Duty of Ministers* (Boston, 1741), p. 19.

15. Edward Holyoke, "The First Sermon for the Dudleian Lecture" (1755), pp. 3, 23–24. MS, Harvard University Archives (H.U.A.).

16. *Ibid.*, pp. 13–14, 27.

17. Shipton, *Sibley*, Vol. VI (Boston, 1942), pp. 59–66.

18. Ebenezer Gay, *Natural Religion, as Distinguished from Revealed* (Boston, 1759), pp. 6–7, 11.

19. Shipton, *Sibley*, Vol. V, pp. 616–623.

20. Peter Clark, *Man's Dignity and Duty as a Reasonable Creature* (Boston, 1763), p. 20.

21. Shipton, *Sibley*, Vol. IX (Boston, 1956), pp. 500–508.

22. Samuel Cooke, "Mr Cooke's Sermon at the annual Dudleian Lecture" (1767), p. 3. MS, H.U.A.

23. Holyoke, Dudleian Lecture, pp. 27–28.

24. Gay, *Natural Religion*, p. 24.

25. Clark, *Man's Dignity*, p. 33.

26. David Barnes, "Revealed Religion" (1780), p. 3. MS, H.U.A. For a biographical sketch of Barnes, see Shipton, *Sibley*, Vol. XIII (Boston, 1965), pp. 189–194.

27. Gay, *Natural Religion*, pp. 19–20.

28. Shipton, *Sibley*, Vol. IV, pp. 501–514.

29. Barnes, "Revealed Religion," pp. 6–7.

30. Thomas Barnard, *The Power of God, the Proof of Christianity* (Salem, 1768), p. 14. For a biographical sketch of Barnard, see Shipton, *Sibley*, Vol. IX, pp. 120–129.

31. J. Barnard, *Proof of Jesus Christ*, pp. 9, 27.

32. T. Barnard, *Power of God*, p. 22.

33. For an indication of the persistence of these ideas in the Campbellite tradition, see Thomas H. Olbricht, "The Rationalism of the Restoration," *Restoration Quarterly*, Vol. XI (1968), pp. 77–88, especially pp. 77–82.

34. Increase Mather, *A Discourse Proving that the Christian Religion Is the Only True Religion* (Boston, 1702). The contents of the book are described in Thomas J. Holmes, *Increase Mather: a Bibliography of His Works*, 2 vols. (Cleveland, 1931), Vol. I, pp. 183–186.

35. John Wise, *A Vindication of the Government of New-England Churches* (Boston, 1717), p. 32.

36. Timothy Dwight, *Theology; Explained and Defended in a Series of Sermons* (Middletown, Conn., 1818), Vol. II, p. 463.

37. See Conrad Wright, *The Beginnings of Unitarianism in America* (Boston, c. 1955), Chap. VI.

38. Alden Bradford, *Memoir of the Life and Writings of Rev. Jonathan Mayhew, D.D.* (Boston, 1838), p. 98.

39. William Bentley, *A Sermon, Preached at the Stone Chapel in Boston* (Boston, 1790), p. 17.

40. *The Works of William E. Channing, D.D.* (Boston, 1841), Vol. III, p. 106.

41. Samuel Johnson, "The Necessity of Revealed Religion," in Herbert and Carol Schneider, eds., *Samuel Johnson, President of King's College* (New York, 1929), Vol. III, pp. 370, 373.

42. Jonathan Dickinson, *The Reasonableness of Christianity* (Boston, 1732), p. 27.

43. Samuel Davies, *Sermons on Important Subjects,* New Edition, in three volumes (London, 1792), Vol. I, p. 57.

44. *The Works of the Rev. John Witherspoon,* 4 vols. (Philadelphia, 1801), Vol. IV, pp. 9–123.

Chapter II: The Rediscovery of Channing: Pages 22–40

1. Robert Leet Patterson, *The Philosophy of William Ellery Channing* (New York, 1952); David P. Edgell, *William Ellery Channing: an Intellectual Portrait* (Boston, c. 1955); Arthur W. Brown, *Always Young for Liberty: a Biography of William Ellery Channing* (Syracuse, N.Y., c. 1956); Madeleine Hooke Rice, *Federal Street Pastor* (New York, c. 1961); Arthur W. Brown, *William Ellery Channing* (New York, c. 1961).

2. Conrad Wright, "A Channing Bibliography: 1929–1959," *Proceedings of the Unitarian Historical Society,* Vol. XII, Pt. 2 (1959), pp. 22–24.

3. Herbert W. Schneider, "The Intellectual Background of William Ellery Channing," *Church History,* Vol. VII (1938), pp. 4, 4n.

4. *Ibid.,* pp. 11, 21.

5. For a briefer but essentially unmodified version of the same position, see Herbert W. Schneider, *A History of American Philosophy* (New York, 1946), pp. 61–63.

6. Patterson, *Philosophy of Channing,* pp. 15, 16. It might be mentioned that on page 16 Patterson has misunderstood Chadwick's discussion of Channing's early tendencies towards Calvinism, and has incorrectly accused him of misrepresenting Channing on this point.

7. Edgell, *Channing,* pp. 98, 81, 18.

8. William H. Channing, *Memoir of William Ellery Channing* (Boston, 1848), Vol. I, p. 33.

9. *The Works of William Ellery Channing* (Boston, 1846), Vol. IV, p. 341.

10. Franklin B. Dexter, *Biographical Sketches of the Graduates of Yale College* (New York, 1885–1912), Vol. IV, pp. 183–186; William B. Sprague, *Annals of the American Pulpit* (New York, 1857–69), Vol. VIII, p. 361; Frances M. Caulkins, *History of New London, Connecticut* (New London, 1852), p. 589.

11. "Library Charging-Lists" in Harvard University Archives.

12. Channing, *Memoir*, Vol. I, p. 73. Channing's concern for Christian evidences reveals his indebtedness to the tradition of Supernatural Rationalism, discussed in the previous essay of the present book.

13. *Ibid.*, Vol. I, pp. 122–123.

14. *Ibid.*, Vol. I, p. 137.

15. William Allen, *Memoir of John Codman, D.D.* (Boston, 1853), pp. 267–268.

16. Channing, *Memoir*, Vol. I, pp. 345, 346, 348–349.

17. Hamilton A. Hill, *History of the Old South Church* (Boston, 1890), Vol. II, p. 285.

18. William Ellery Channing, *A Sermon Delivered at the Ordination of the Rev. John Codman* (Boston, 1808), p. 16; compare Henry Ware, *An Inquiry into the Foundation, Evidences, and Truths of Religion* (Cambridge, 1842), Vol. II, p. 267.

19. Emily Ellsworth Fowler Ford, *Notes on the Life of Noah Webster*, 2 vols. (New York, 1912), Vol. II, p. 72.

20. "Memoirs" of John Pierce, Vol. I, p. 263. MS, Massachusetts Historical Society. After Channing's death, Pierce recalled how difficult it had been for his contemporaries to know precisely what his theological convictions were in the very first years of his ministry: "At this period, and for several subsequent years, he was conservative, to the highest degree. He preached no controversial sermons. He associated more with those who called themselves orthodox, than with any other denomination. Indeed, christians of this stamp thronged to his house of worship, and helped to fill his Church. Indeed so cautious was he, on points of difference, that, for several years, when I was in the habit of ranging the Congregational ministers of this Commonwealth under 4 heads, Hopkinsian, Calvinist, Arminian, and doubtful, I felt obliged to place him among the doubtful. This however was always observable, that he never closed his prayers with a Trinitarian ascription." "Memoirs" of John Pierce, Vol. IX, pp. 533–534.

21. John Ware, *Memoir of the Life of Henry Ware, Jr.* (Boston, 1846), p. 48.

22. *Ibid.*, pp. 49–50.

23. Channing, *Memoir*, Vol. I, p. 161.

24. *Ibid.*, Vol. I, pp. 344–345.

25. Edgell, *Channing*, pp. 148–149.

26. Schneider, *American Philosophy*, p. 262; John E. Dirks, *The Critical Theology of Theodore Parker* (New York, 1948), p. 136; H. Shelton Smith, "Was Theodore Parker a Transcendentalist?" *New England Quarterly*, Vol. XXIII (1950), p. 363.

27. Arthur R. Schultz and Henry A. Pochman, "George Ripley: Unitarian, Transcendentalist, or Infidel?" *American Literature*, Vol. XIV (1942), p. 19.

28. Harold C. Goddard, *Studies in New England Transcendentalism* (New York, 1908), p. 28.

29. Arthur I. Ladu, "Channing and Transcendentalism," *American Literature*, Vol. XI (1939), pp. 136–137.

30. Ralph L. Rusk, ed., *The Letters of Ralph Waldo Emerson* (New York, 1939), Vol. I, pp. 412–413.

31. John Weiss, *Discourse Occasioned by the Death of Convers Francis, D.D.* (Cambridge, 1863), pp. 28–29.

32. Rusk, *Letters of Emerson*, Vol. I, p. 413.

33. Ladu, *op. cit.*, Vol. XI, p. 132.

34. Smith, *op. cit.*, Vol. XXIII, p. 354.

35. Channing, *Works*, Vol. III, p. 240.

36. Goddard, *Studies*, p. 27.

37. Walter Fuller Taylor, *A History of American Letters* (Boston and New York, 1936), p. 142.

38. Rod W. Horton and Herbert W. Edwards, *Backgrounds of American Literary Thought* (New York, 1952), p. 109.

Chapter III: Emerson, Barzillai Frost, and the Divinity School Address: Pages 41–61

1. *Journals of Ralph Waldo Emerson* (Boston, 1909–1914), Vol. IV, pp. 188–189.

2. Emerson himself regarded Ware as one of the most eloquent of the Boston preachers. See *Journals*, Vol. VI, pp. 455–456; Vol. VII, p. 170.

3. Concord *Yeoman's Gazette*, Feb. 4, 1837.

4. Henry Frost, "Barzillai Frost," in *Memoirs of Members of the Social Circle in Concord*, 3rd Ser. (Cambridge, 1907); also Henry A. Miles, *A Sermon Preached in the First Parish Church, Concord, December 10, 1858, at the Burial of Rev. Barzillai Frost* (Cambridge, 1859).

5. Concord *Freeman*, March 11, 1837.

6. Emerson's manuscript "Preaching Record" shows that he preached in East Lexington in February, March, and April, every Sunday except as follows: Feb. 19, at Waltham, William Silsbee at East Lexington; Feb. 26, C. A. Bartol at East Lexington; March 19, at Waltham; March 26, at Lowell; April 16, in the afternoon at West Lexington; April 23, at Wayland; April 30, at Watertown. The "Preaching Record," like the manuscript Journals, is deposited in the Harvard College Library; both have been used by courtesy of Mr. E. W. Forbes and the Emerson Memorial Association. See also R. L. Rusk, *The Letters of Ralph Waldo Emerson* (New York, 1939), Vol. II, pp. 68, 71–72, 73.

7. *Journals*, Vol. IV, p. 232. Although citations will be made to the printed *Journals*, all quotations in this paper have been corrected, and when necessary enlarged, by reference to the original manuscript.

8. *Journals*, Vol. IV, pp. 229–230.

9. *Ibid.*, Vol. IV, pp. 232–233. With this passage, compare the corresponding part of the Divinity School Address in *Works* (Boston, 1903), Vol. I, p. 138.

10. *Journals*, Vol. IV, p. 244.

11. Miles, *Sermon at the Burial of Barzillai Frost*, pp. 9, 11; *Journals*, Vol. IV, p. 244.

12. Miles, *Sermon*, p. 16.

13. *Ibid.*, pp. 10, 12–13, 14.

14. Emerson, *Works*, Vol. X, p. 282.

15. "Preaching Record"; Rusk, *Letters*, Vol. II, pp. 79–81, 83, 85, 88; Stanley Williams, "Unpublished Letters of Emerson," *Journal of English and Germanic Philology*, Vol. XXVI (1927), p. 476; *Yeoman's Gazette*, July 8, 1837. The "Preaching Record" shows that Emerson was at East Lexington every Sunday except as follows: July 23, at Framingham; Aug. 13, when Hedge preached for him; Aug. 20, at Waltham; Aug. 27; Sept. 3 (?); Oct. 1, Richard Austin at E. Lexington; Oct. 8, at Waltham; Oct. 15, at Billerica; Nov. 12, at Waltham; Nov. 19, at Concord; Nov. 26, at Weston.

16. *Journals*, Vol. IV, pp. 300–301, 324.

17. Miles, *Sermon at the Burial of Barzillai Frost*, pp. 10–11.

18. A. C. McGiffert, Jr., *Young Emerson Speaks* (Boston, 1938), pp. 120–126; Rusk, *Letters*, Vol. I, pp. 412–413; J. E. Cabot, *A Memoir of Ralph Waldo Emerson* (Boston, 1887), Vol. II, pp. 726–728.

19. Miles, *Sermon at the Burial of Barzillai Frost*, p. 6.

20. Rusk, *Letters*, Vol. II, p. 103; Emerson, *Journals*, Vol. IV, pp. 377, 379. Compare *Works*, Vol. I, p. 143. In the printed *Journals*, the paragraph beginning "Whilst meditating on the ideal" is incorrectly dated December 8 instead of December 3. In the manuscript Journal, the name of Emerson's uncle has been expanded at a later date to read: Mr S. Ripley.

21. Rusk, *Letters*, Vol. II, pp. 108, 113.

22. Rusk, *Letters*, Vol. II, p. 114; *Journals*, Vol. I, p. 363. See also Henry Nash Smith, "Emerson's Problem of Vocation," *New England Quarterly*, Vol. XII (1939), pp. 52–67; and Stephen E. Whicher, *Freedom and Fate* (Philadelphia, 1953).

23. Rusk, *Letters*, Vol. II, p. 120; *Journals*, Vol. V, pp. 280–281.

24. The manuscript "Preaching Record" shows that Emerson preached in 1838 and 1839 as follows: Feb. 4, 1838, Concord; Feb. 11, Concord; Feb. 18, E. Lexington; Feb. 25, E. Lexington; March 25, E. Lexington (Sermons 154, "Duty," and 87, "Self-Culture," enlarged by lecture on religion); April 5, Fast Day at E. Lexington and Concord ("Peace Lecture"); April 8, New York (Sermons 154 and 87 enlarged); April 29, Waltham (Sermons 37 and 87 enlarged); Aug. 15, Watertown (Sermons 154 and 87 enlarged); Jan. 13, 1839, Concord (Sermons 101 and 87 enlarged); Jan. 20, Concord (Sermon 169). January 20, 1839, is the last entry in the "Preaching Record." Several of these sermons, preached at the close of Emerson's pulpit activity, are among those reprinted in McGiffert, *Young Emerson Speaks*.

25. *Journals*, Vol. IV, pp. 402, 412–413; compare *Works*, Vol. I, pp. 137–139, 145.

26. For the letter from the committee to Emerson, see Rusk, *Letters*, Vol. II, p. 147. Rusk does not list Emerson's reply, but it was copied into "The Records of the Theological School" (the "Student History"), MS, Andover-Harvard Library. In later years, Emerson took pains to reject the title of "Reverend" when correspondents mistakenly used it. See Rusk, *Letters*, Vol. IV, pp. 115, 173; Vol. V, p. 183.

27. *Journals*, Vol. IV, pp. 420, 423, 427–429.

28. *Ibid.*, Vol. IV, pp. 454–455; compare *Works*, Vol. I, p. 146.

29. *Journals*, Vol. IV, p. 455; compare *Works*, Vol. I, pp. 146–147.

30. The manuscript as well as the printed *Journals* date this entry May 26. For about three weeks, Emerson was mistaken as to the date. The entry describing "our pretty country church music" is given in the manuscript under the date of June 9, instead of June 10; and the pages beginning with the entry on Napoleon and means and ends are dated "16 June, Sunday" instead of June 17. By the following Saturday, June 23, he was back on the right calendar again. See *Journals*, Vol. IV, pp. 457, 468, 477, 491.

31. *Journals*, Vol. IV, p. 457. Hedge was one of Emerson's close friends, yet Emerson somehow felt that "there is always a fence betwixt us." See Rusk, *Letters*, Vol. II, p. 270; Vol. III, p. 53.

32. *Journals*, Vol. IV, pp. 234, 478, 480–481.

33. *Journals*, Vol. IV, pp. 494, 496; compare *Works*, Vol. I, pp. 137, 139.

34. *Journals*, Vol. V, p. 4.

35. McGiffert, *Young Emerson Speaks*, pp. 36–45, 265.

36. *Journals*, Vol. IV, p. 454; *Works*, Vol. I, pp. 137, 145.

37. See my chapter in G. H. Williams, ed., *The Harvard Divinity School* (Boston, 1954).

38. *Journals*, Vol. V, pp. 7, 9–10.

39. Ferris Greenslet, *James Russell Lowell* (Boston, 1905), p. 23; T. W. Higginson, *Old Cambridge* (New York, 1899), pp. 156–157; E. E. Hale, *James Russell Lowell and His Friends* (Boston, 1899), p. 42.

40. Lowell to G. B. Loring, July 8, 1838; MS, Harvard College Library, also in C. E. Norton, ed., *Letters of James Russell Lowell* (Boston, 1904), Vol. I, p. 28; H. E. Scudder, *James Russell Lowell* (Boston, 1901), Vol. I, p. 54; Moorfield Storey and Edward W. Emerson, *Ebenezer Rockwood Hoar* (Boston, 1911), pp. 30–32.

41. Nathan Hale, Jr., to Lowell, July 9, 1838, MS, Harvard College Library (H.C.L.).

42. Hale to Lowell, June 29, 1838, H.C.L.; see also Hale, *James Russell Lowell*, p. 47. Frost was married on June 1, 1837, in Framingham to Miss Elmira Stone of that town; see *Yeoman's Gazette*, June 3, 1837.

43. Lowell to G. B. Loring, July 1, 1838, H.C.L.; also Scudder, *Lowell*, Vol. I, pp. 51–52; Hale, *Lowell*, p. 46.

44. Hale, *Lowell*, p. 45.

45. Whicher, *Freedom and Fate*, p. 73.

46. *Journals*, Vol. V, pp. 20, 28, 45, 160, 167, 171, 173, 180–182, 197, 200.

47. *Journals*, Vol. V, pp. 265, 269, 271, 407.

48. Edward Waldo Emerson, *Emerson in Concord* (Boston, 1889), p. 169; Rusk, *Letters*, Vol. IV, pp. 289, 326, 339.

49. Frost to Emerson, June 1839, MS, H.C.L., summarized in Rusk, *Letters*, Vol. II, pp. 207n–208n; Frost to Emerson, April 17, 1841, H.C.L.; Nathaniel Hawthorne, *The American Notebooks*, ed. Randall Stewart (New Haven, 1932), p.

165; Frost to Emerson, Jan. 5, 1847, H.C.L.; Rusk, *Letters,* Vol. IV, pp. 125, 405, 426.

50. Miles, *Sermon at the Burial of Barzillai Frost,* pp. 17–22; *Memoirs of Members of the Social Circle in Concord,* pp. 56–58. Frost's will, signed on Feb. 4, 1856, was witnessed by Samuel Hoar, John Thoreau (the father), and Henry D. Thoreau.

51. E. W. Emerson, *Emerson in Concord,* p. 191.

Chapter IV: The Minister as Reformer: Pages 62–80

1. George Willis Cooke, *Unitarianism in America* (Boston, 1902), p. 353.

2. Samuel J. May, *Some Recollections of Our Antislavery Conflict* (Boston, 1869), pp. 335, 337.

3. John Haynes Holmes, "Unitarians and the Social Question," *The Unitarian,* Vol. III (1908), p. 432.

4. Henry W. Bellows spent the winter of 1837–38 in Mobile, was urged to stay, and was tempted with a handsome salary, "but the awful shadow of slavery frightened him away." See Russell N. Bellows, "Henry Whitney Bellows," in T. B. Peck, *The Bellows Genealogy* (Keene, N.H., 1898), p. 286. George F. Simmons was invited to serve the Mobile church in 1839, and went there with the understanding that he was not proslavery; but when he delivered two antislavery sermons, two gentlemen of the church waited on him to suggest "that if he consulted his personal safety, he would leave as speedily as possible." *The Liberator,* Vol. X (1840), p. 105; see also pp. 99, 111, 115. Mellish I. Motte was sent to Savannah in 1843 to supply the pulpit temporarily, but did not preach even one Sunday because, though a Southerner by birth, and no Garrisonian, he had once preached against racial prejudice. *The Liberator,* Vol. XIII (1843), pp. 40, 53; see also A. P. Peabody in the *Christian Examiner,* Vol. XXXIV (1843), p. 268.

5. G. W. Cooke thought that Clapp was perhaps a Universalist and so the antislavery record of the Unitarians was clear; but Clapp became a Unitarian on abandoning the Presbyterian church in 1834, and was listed as such for twenty years in the *Unitarian Register.* For his defense of slavery, see Theodore Clapp, *Slavery: a Sermon, Delivered . . . April 15, 1838* (New Orleans, 1838); also *Autobiographical Sketches and Recollections* (Boston, 1857), pp. 341–343, 378–379. More obscure than Clapp was Charles M. Taggart, who died in 1853 in his early thirties, of whom his biographer said: "upon the vexed question of slavery, he held opinions not shared by a large portion of his Unitarian brethren, some of whom may have thought that a Southern residence had unduly biassed his mind." See John H. Heywood, "Memoir," prefixed to Charles M. Taggart, *Sermons* (Boston, 1856), p. lviii.

6. "Rev. Theodore Clapp, of New-Orleans, is said to be an apologist and defender of slavery, the only Unitarian minister in the country who openly takes this ground." *Thirteenth Annual Report of the American and Foreign Anti-Slavery Society* (New York, 1853), p. 107.

7. The following Unitarian ministers were thanked in 1858 by the Executive Committee of the American Anti-Slavery Society for having assisted as public speakers and in other ways: T. W. Higginson, Theodore Parker, J. T. Sargent, D. A. Wasson, Frederick Frothingham, S. J. May, W. H. Fish, O. B. Frothingham, W. H Furness, and M. D. Conway. *Annual Reports of the American Anti-Slavery Society . . . for the Years Ending May 1, 1857, and May 1, 1858* (New York, 1859), p. 188.

8. A number of Unitarian ministers were colonizationists in the early days who were quite willing to forget it later. In 1833, more than thirty students of the Harvard Divinity School supported a resolution commending the Colonization Society for its effectiveness as leading to the entire abolition of slavery; among them were James Freeman Clarke and Barzillai Frost, who afterwards were abolitionists. See *The Colonizationist and Journal of Freedom* (Boston, 1833–34), p. 35. The following Unitarian ministers were listed as life members of the American Colonization Society in 1832: Nathan Parker, Orville Dewey, James Kendall, John Allyn, Convers Francis. [American Colonization Society], *Fifteenth Annual Report of the American Society for Colonizing the Free People of Colour* (Washington, 1832), p. 53. Other supporters of colonization at that time were: O. W. B. Peabody, R. C. Waterston, E. S. Gannett, F. Parkman, E. Ripley, F. W. Holland, and J. Pierpont. See *The Colonizationist and Journal of Freedom* (1833–34), pp. 11, 12, 67, 130, 132, 196, 358.

9. Samuel J. May, *A Brief Account of His Ministry* (Syracuse, N.Y., 1867), pp. 10, 47; also *Memoir of Samuel Joseph May* (Boston, 1873), pp. 69–70.

10. May, *Some Recollections*, p. 19.

11. *The Liberator*, Vol. I (1831), pp. 87, 106, 118.

12. *Proceedings of the Anti-Slavery Convention, Assembled at Philadelphia, December 4, 5, and 6, 1833* (New York, 1833).

13. May, *Some Recollections*, pp. 39–51; S. J. May, *The Right of Colored People to Education, Vindicated* (Brooklyn, Conn., 1833); *The Liberator*, Vols. III (1833) and IV (1834), *passim*. For a recent retelling of the story, see Edwin W. and Miriam R. Small, "Prudence Crandall: Champion of Negro Education," *New England Quarterly*, Vol. XVII (1944), pp. 506–529.

14. May, *Right of Colored People*, p. 8n.

15. Joseph May, *Samuel Joseph May: a Memorial Study* (Boston, 1898), pp. 14–15.

16. *Twelfth Annual Report Presented to the Massachusetts Anti-Slavery Society* (Boston, 1844), pp. 76, 78.

17. *The Liberator*, Vol. VIII (1838), p. 186.

18. *Ibid.*, Vol. XX (1850), pp. 14, 17.

19. *Ibid.*, Vol. IX (1839), p. 164. The reference in this case was to the New-England Non-Resistance Society.

20. Samuel J. May, *A Discourse on Slavery in the United States* (Boston, 1832).

21. *Ibid.*, p. 20. May's proposal here is not spelled out in detail; apparently he was suggesting not compensation to all slaveholders for the loss of their investment, but simply financial aid to those who would otherwise be virtually ruined.

22. *The Liberator*, Vol. VIII (1838), p. 3.

23. *Ibid.*, Vol. XXI (1851), p. 81. In 1836, May's position was that "the framers of our Constitution finding they had not the power to abolish slavery, were determined to do the next best thing—*not commit the national government to its support.*" See Samuel J. May, "Slavery and the Constitution," *Quarterly Anti-Slavery Magazine*, Vol. II (1836–37), p. 89. The essay was printed in the magazine in two parts, Vol. II, pp. 73–90 and 226–238.

24. Samuel J. May, "The Liberty Bell is Not of the Liberty Party," *The Liberator*, Vol. XV (1845), p. 13.

25. S. J. May to S. May, Jr., in *The Liberator*, Vol. XVIII (1848), p. 135.

26. Samuel J. May, *Liberty or Slavery, the Only Question* (Syracuse, N.Y., 1856), p. 30.

27. The Reverend Samuel May, Jr., of Leicester, was the General Agent of the Anti-Slavery Society from 1847 to 1865; the Reverend Frederick W. Holland was Secretary of the Unitarian Association from 1848 to 1850. The importance of family connections for the study of American Unitarianism in the nineteenth century should not be overlooked. The Reverend Joseph May, the son of Samuel J. May, was the minister in Philadelphia for twenty-five years. The Reverend Frederick May Holland, the son of Frederick W. Holland, served churches in Illinois, Ohio, and Wisconsin. The niece of Samuel May, Jr., married the Reverend Christopher R. Eliot; his son, Dr. Frederick May Eliot, was as conscious of, and as proud of, his inheritance on this side of the family as of his more obvious Eliot connections.

28. *Christian Inquirer*, June 7, 1851. The text of May's resolution is in S. J. May, *Some Recollections*, pp. 368–369. For May's justification of himself, see S. J. May to E. S. Gannett, August 7, 1851, Gannett Papers, Massachusetts Historical Society.

29. [Massachusetts Anti-Slavery Society], *Fifth Annual Report* (Boston, 1837), p. xxxi.

30. "Rev. Dr. Bellows," *Harper's Weekly*, Vol. III (1859), p. 549.

31. Cyrus A. Bartol, "Henry W. Bellows," *Unitarian Review*, Vol. XVII (1882), p. 234. M.H.S.

32. Bellows to Bartol, Nov. 1, 1848, Bellows Papers, Massachusetts Historical Society.

33. Henry W. Bellows, *The First Congregational Church in the City of New York* (New York, 1899), pp. 25–26.

34. *Christian Inquirer*, Jan. 19, 1850.

35. [American Anti-Slavery Society], *Annual Report* (New York, 1855), pp. 145–147.

36. George F. Simmons to Bellows, Nov. 8, 1845. M.H.S.

37. *Christian Inquirer*, Dec. 22, 1849.

38. Bellows to Bartol, March 9, 1850. M.H.S.

39. *Christian Inquirer*, March 16, 1850.

40. Bellows to Bartol, March 25, 1850. M.H.S.

41. *Christian Inquirer*, Nov. 13, 1852.

42. *Ibid.*, March 16, 1850.

43. *Ibid.*, Nov. 15, 1856.

44. *Ibid.,* Jan. 27, 1857. A partial text of Bellows's letter may also be found in *Proceedings of the State Disunion Convention* (Boston, 1857), "Appendix," pp. 17–18.

45. *Christian Inquirer,* Jan. 12, 1861.

46. *Ibid.,* April 20, 1861.

47. From the Dedham *Gazette,* quoted in *The Liberator,* Vol. XXII (1852), p. 26.

48. Mary E. Dewey, ed., *Autobiography and Letters of Orville Dewey, D.D.* (Boston, 1883), p. 129; Orville Dewey, "On American Morals and Manners," *Christian Examiner,* Vol. XXXVI (1844), p. 267n.

49. Orville Dewey, *Moral Views of Commerce, Society and Politics,* 2nd ed. (New York, 1838), p. 286.

50. Orville Dewey, *A Discourse on Slavery and the Annexation of Texas* (New York, 1844).

51. M. E. Dewey, *Orville Dewey,* p. 192.

52. Orville Dewey, *Discourses on the Nature of Religion,* Vol. II of *Works of Orville Dewey* (New York, 1847), p. 369.

53. *Ibid.,* p. 371.

54. May, *Some Recollections,* pp. 368–369.

55. *The Liberator,* Vol. XXI (1851), p. 90.

56. Orville Dewey, *The Laws of Human Progress and Modern Reforms* (New York, 1852), p. 24; for the full text of the controversial address, see the *Christian Inquirer,* Jan. 18, 1851.

57. Dewey, *Laws of Human Progress,* p. 28.

58. M. E. Dewey, *Orville Dewey,* pp. 241–242; see also William J. Grayson, *Reply to Dr. Dewey's Address* (Charleston, S.C., 1856).

59. Orville Dewey, *On Patriotism* (Boston, 1859).

60. Orville Dewey, *A Sermon, Preached on the National Fast Day* (Boston, 1861), p. 21.

61. Bellows to Bartol, March 25, 1850. M.H.S.

Chapter V: Henry W. Bellows and the Organization of the National Conference: Pages 81–109

1. The account most commonly used by historians, the one by Stow Persons, relies largely on sources unfriendly to Bellows: Stow Persons, *Free Religion* (New Haven, 1947), esp. Chap. I. Frank Walker, on the other hand, has taken exception to Persons's treatment, suggesting that Bellows's motives have been misunderstood and his theology incorrectly categorized. Walker's paper makes use of the Bellows Papers, but does not provide more than a preliminary probe of their riches: Frank Walker, "Ecumenicity and Liberty: the Contribution of Henry W. Bellows to the Development of Post-Civil War Unitarianism," *Proceedings of the Unitarian Historical Society,* Vol. XIII, Pt. II (1961), p. 11.

2. Henry W. Bellows, *The Reformed Church of Christendom, or the Duties of Liberal Christians to the National Faith at this Crisis of Opinions* (Boston, 1865),

p. 14. Bellows had spoken in this vein at least as early as May, 1863. See *Monthly Journal* of the American Unitarian Association, Vol. IV (1863), pp. 335–338.

3. *Report of the Convention of Unitarian Churches Held in New York, on the 5th and 6th of April, 1865* (Boston, 1866), p. ix. See also Bellows, "Popular Creeds and the Nation's Life," *Christian Examiner,* Vol. LXXX (1866), pp. 1–14.

4. Bellows to his sister, Eliza Dorr, Sept. 11, 1864. Massachusetts Historical Society collection of Bellows Papers (M.H.S.).

5. Bellows to Hale, Feb. 15, 1864. M.H.S.

6. Bellows to R. N. Bellows, Dec. 12, 1864. M.H.S.

7. Thornton K. Lothrop, ed., *Some Reminiscences of the Life of Samuel Kirkland Lothrop* (Cambridge, 1888), p. 202.

8. George Willis Cooke, *Unitarianism in America* (Boston, 1902), pp. 158–160.

9. Thus Stow Persons, *Free Religion,* p. 15.

10. Bellows to R. N. Bellows, Dec. 10, 1863. M.H.S.

11. Bellows to Orville Dewey, Jan. 2, 1864. M.H.S. Extensive quotation from this letter, occasioned by the twenty-fifth anniversary of Bellows's ordination, may be found in Thomas Bellows Peck, *The Bellows Genealogy* (Keene, N.H., 1898), esp. pp. 296–298.

12. Cyrus A. Bartol, "Henry Whitney Bellows," *Unitarian Review,* Vol. XVII (1882), p. 234.

13. Bellows to Hale, Dec. 31, 1864. M.H.S.

14. Bellows to R. N. Bellows, March 1, 1865. M.H.S. This letter (though with some errors in transcription) may be found in Walker, *op. cit.,* p. 9. Bellows's criticisms of Boston parochialism were nothing new. See also Bellows, *Unitarianism in Boston: A Friendly Criticism* (New York, 1854). See also comments on Boston apathy in W. H. Savary to Hale, Dec. 8, 1864, and W. T. Clarke to Hale, Dec. 8, 1864. Hale Papers, Harvard Divinity School (H.D.S.).

15. Bellows to R. N. Bellows, March 1, 1865. M.H.S.

16. Bellows to J. F. Clarke, March 23, 1865. M.H.S.

17. Hale to Bellows, Feb. 11, 1864. M.H.S.

18. Bellows to Hedge, Dec. 13, 1864. M.H.S. The mortality rate of the "free churches" organized by radicals—Higginson's in Worcester, Samuel Johnson's in Lynn, Abbot's in Dover, N.H., Frothingham's in Jersey City and New York, even Parker's Twenty-Eighth Congregational Society—gives point to these comments.

19. Bellows to R. N. Bellows, Mar. 1, 1865. M.H.S.

20. Bellows to R. N. Bellows, Mar. 1, 1865. M.H.S.

21. Bellows to Hedge, Dec. 13, 1864. M.H.S.

22. Bellows to Hale, Jan. 16, 1865. M.H.S.

23. Bellows to Hale, Jan. 16, 1865. M.H.S.

24. The opposition of the radicals to creedal formulations was well stated by Francis Ellingwood Abbot in a letter to the *Christian Inquirer* (March 11, 1865).

25. Bellows to Hale, March 17, 1865. M.H.S.

26. Bellows to Clarke, March 23, 1865. M.H.S.

27. Henry W. Bellows, Sermon at the ordination of E. W. Hathaway, *Christian Register* (June 30, 1866).

28. Bellows to R. N. Bellows, March 1, 1865. M.H.S.

29. Bellows, Sermon at the ordination of E. W. Hathaway, *op. cit.*

30. Bellows to Clarke, March 23, 1865. M.H.S. The final shape which these ideas took in Bellows's mind may be seen in: "Christianity and the Church to be Credited on their Merits" (1881), in H. W. Bellows, *Twenty-Four Sermons* (New York, 1886), pp. 366–393.

31. Bellows to Clarke, March 27, 1865. M.H.S.

32. J. F. Clarke, "Union of Churches," *Monthly Journal* of the A.U.A., Vol. V (1864), p. 201.

33. *Monthly Journal,* Vol. V (1864), pp. 313–323, esp. pp. 319–320.

34. William J. Potter, "The War and Liberal Theology," *Monthly Journal,* Vol. VI (1865), pp. 65–79.

35. *Monthly Journal,* Vol. V (1864), pp. 477–478.

36. *Monthly Journal,* Vol. V (1864), pp. 525, 569.

37. Lowe to Bellows, Oct. 25, 1864. M.H.S.

38. A detailed report of the meeting appeared in the *Christian Register* (Dec. 10, 1864); it was reprinted in the *Christian Inquirer* (Dec. 17, 1864), and later used as the basis for the official report in the *Monthly Journal,* Vol. VI (1865), pp. 1–20. For evidence as to the enthusiasm sparked by Bellows's resolution, see also: "How the Matter Stands," *Christian Inquirer* (Dec. 31, 1864).

39. For biographical sketches of Low and Pratt, see the *Dictionary of American Biography.*

40. Bellows to Hale, Jan. 11, 1865. M.H.S.

41. Bellows to R. N. Bellows, Dec. 12, 1864. M.H.S.

42. Bellows to R. N. Bellows, Jan. 21, 1865. M.H.S.

43. Brigham to Bellows, Jan. 13, 1865. M.H.S.

44. W. T. Clarke to Hale, Jan. 24, 1865. M.H.S.

45. Bellows to Thomas Hill, Jan. 18, 1865; to A. A. Livermore, Feb. 6, 1865. M.H.S.

46. J. H. Allen to Bellows, Jan. 20, 1865. M.H.S.

47. This drive for funds was successful, and yielded more than $111,000. *Monthly Journal,* Vol. VI (1865), p. 294.

48. Bellows to Hale, Jan. 16, 1865. M.H.S.

49. The date chosen threatened to conflict with the traditional observance of Fast Day in Massachusetts; but Governor Andrew neatly solved that problem by fixing a day later in the month for the public holiday. See Hedge to Hale, Feb. 8, 1865. H.D.S.

50. The report was printed both in the *Register* and the *Inquirer* (Feb. 4, 1865). Bellows's grandest vision of what the Liberal Church of America might be was reserved for his own family: Bellows to R. N. Bellows, Jan. 30, 1865. M.H.S.

51. Hale to Bellows, Jan. 11, 1865. M.H.S. W. T. Clarke of Chelsea was especially active in helping Hale round up support. Clark to Hale, Feb. 15, 1865. H.D.S.

52. Bellows, *The Reformed Church of Christendom, or the Duties of Liberal Christians to the National Faith at this Crisis of Opinions* (Boston, 1865).

53. Reprinted in *Report of the Convention,* pp. vi–xi.

54. Hale to Bellows, Jan. 12, 1865. M.H.S.

55. A. B. Ellis, *Memoir of Rufus Ellis* (Boston, 1891), p. 182.

56. Hale to Bellows, March 10, 1865. M.H.S.

57. Henry B. Rogers to Bellows, March 20, 1865. M.H.S.

58. Bartol to Bellows, April 9, 1865; Bellows to Bartol, April 12, 1865. M.H.S.

59. Frothingham was still sore about it in 1891, when he published in his auto-biography a curiously distorted account of it, which cannot be reconciled with the original correspondence. See O. B. Frothingham, *Recollections and Impressions,* 1822–1890 (New York, 1891), pp. 118–19, with which may be compared: S. Osgood to Bellows, Dec. 19, 1863; Frothingham to Bellows, Dec. 24, 1863; Osgood to Bellows, Dec. 25, 1863; Bellows to R. N. Bellows, Dec. 25, 1863; Frothingham to Bellows, Dec. 30, 1863; Bellows to Frothingham, Dec. 30, 1863; Frothingham to Bellows, Dec. 31, 1863; all at M.H.S.

60. Bellows to R. N. Bellows, Feb. 11, 1865. M.H.S.

61. Bellows to R. N. Bellows, March 1, 1865. M.H.S.

62. Hale to Bellows, March 15, 1865. M.H.S. See also W. T. Clarke to Hale, March 15, 1865. H.D.S.

63. Bellows to Hale, March 28, 1865. M.H.S.

64. Bellows to Hale, March 17, 1865. M.H.S.

65. Bellows to Clarke, March 23, 1865. M.H.S.

66. Bellows to Hale, March 17, 1865. M.H.S.

67. A. A. Livermore to Bellows, March 11, 1865. M.H.S.

68. *Christian Inquirer,* March 11, 1865; Bellows to Hale, March 13, 1865. M.H.S.

69. Bellows to Hale, March 27, 1865. M.H.S.

70. Hale to Bellows, March 27, 1865. M.H.S.

71. Mrs. Bellows to Eliza Dorr, March 21, 1865. M.H.S.

72. Anna L. Bellows to R. N. Bellows, April 11, 1865. M.H.S.

73. *Report of the Convention,* pp. 3–32.

74. Anna L. Bellows to R. N. Bellows, April 11, 1865. M.H.S.

75. Anna L. Bellows to R. N. Bellows, April 11, 1865. M.H.S.

76. John White Chadwick, *Henry W. Bellows: His Life and Character. A Sermon* (New York, 1882), pp. 18–19.

77. Anna L. Bellows to R. N. Bellows, April 11, 1865. M.H.S.

78. Bellows to Hale, March 28, 1865. M.H.S.

79. Hale to Bellows, March 25, 1865; Bellows to Hale, March 17, 1865. M.H.S.

80. E. C. Towne, *Unitarian Fellowship and Liberty* (Cambridge, 1866), p. 7.

81. *Report of the Convention,* pp. 46–48.

82. Bellows to Hale, March 17, 1865. M.H.S.

83. A reasonably detailed description of the proceedings, with summaries of remarks by important speakers in debate, was printed in both the *Inquirer* and the *Register* (April 15, 1865). Towne's pamphlet gives additional details.

84. *Christian Register,* April 15, 1865.

85. Bellows to R. N. Bellows, April 12, 1865. M.H.S.

86. O. B. Frothingham, "The Unitarian Convention and the Times," *Friend of Progress,* Vol. I (1864–65), pp. 225–230; afterwards reprinted as a tract.

87. "The Unitarian Convention," *Friend of Progress,* Vol. I (1864–65), pp. 208–09.

88. "The Two Confederacies," *Christian Register* (June 24, 1865).

89. For the Syracuse meeting, see the *Christian Inquirer* (October 18, 1866); J. F. Clarke and F. E. Abbot, *The Battle of Syracuse* (Boston, 1884); and Stow Persons, *Free Religion.* On Abbot's career, the fullest treatment is by Sydney E. Ahlstrom, *Francis Ellingwood Abbot,* unpublished dissertation, Harvard, 1951.

90. Towne, *Unitarian Fellowship,* esp. pp. 6–17.

91. Allen to Bellows, Dec. 21, 1865. M.H.S.

92. Bellows to Allen, Nov. 11, 1865; Allen to Bellows, Nov. 13, 1865. M.H.S.

93. Allen to Bellows, Jan. 4, 1866. M.H.S. Two years later, Bellows persuaded Towne to resubmit the article. See E. C. Towne, "Christianity and Pseudo-Christianity," *Christian Examiner,* Vol. LXXXII (1867), pp. 133–160.

94. For a judgment on the convention by a radical who did not attend, see Samuel Johnson, "Bond or Free," in *The Radical.* James Freeman Clarke responded to Johnson's attack on his sermon, and an interchange followed, which soon diverged from the question of the convention to other issues. See *The Radical,* Vol. I (1865–66), pp. 49–59; 148–152; 218–226; 342–347.

95. A. D. Mayo to Hale, Jan. 4, 1865. Hale Papers, H.D.S.

96. W. W. Newell to Hale, April 24, 1865. Hale Papers, H.D.S.

97. Frederic Henry Hedge, "Memorial Address," Appendix to J. H. Allen, *Our Liberal Movement in Theology* (Boston, 1882), p. 204.

98. J. W. Chadwick, *Henry W. Bellows,* p. 19.

99. C. A. Bartol, "Henry Whitney Bellows," *Unitarian Review,* Vol. XVII (1882), p. 238.

Chapter VI: From Standing Order to Secularism: Pages 110–123

1. Conrad Wright, "Piety, Morality, and the Commonwealth," *Crane Review,* Vol. IX (1967), pp. 90–106.

2. W. E. Channing, *Religion a Social Principle* (Boston, 1820), pp. 10, 11, 14. A part of this sermon, entitled: "Importance of Religion to Society," excluding the application to the political issues of 1820, may be found in Channing's collected works.

3. *An Answer to a Piece, Entitled "An Appeal to the Impartial Publick . . ."* (Salem, 1785), pp. 12–13.

4. *Ibid.,* pp. 17–18.

5. *An Appeal to the Impartial Public by The Society of Christian Independents, Congregating in Glocester* (Boston, 1785), p. 20.

6. Thus Andrew Preston Peabody, "Defense of the Third Article," *Christian Examiner,* Vol. XIII (1833), pp. 351–363, and Artemas B. Muzzey, *Christian Register,* Vol. XI (1832), pp. 158, 162, 166, 170, 178.

7. "Amendment of the Third Article," *Christian Examiner,* Vol. XIII (1833), pp. 346–347.

8. In this connection, a fascinating article by Ezra Stiles Gannett in 1845 argues that Harvard College should be kept free from sectarian control, and that the way this is to be accomplished is to make sure that the Unitarians control it. Ezra Stiles Gannett, "Harvard College—Sectarianism," *Christian Examiner,* Vol. XXXIX (1845), pp. 261–272.

9. W. E. Channing, "Remarks on Education," *Works* (Boston, 1843), Vol. I, p. 376. (From the *Christian Examiner,* November, 1833.)

10. Cited in Raymond B. Culver, *Horace Mann and Religion in the Massachusetts Public Schools* (New Haven, 1929), p. 22.

11. Cited in William Kailer Dunn, *What Happened to Religious Education?* (Baltimore, 1958), pp. 131–132.

12. This issue comes into sharp focus in *Commonwealth v. Cooke,* 7 Am. L. Reg. 417, conveniently available in Mark DeWolfe Howe, *Cases on Church and State in the United States* (Cambridge, 1952), pp. 316–321.

13. John Webb Pratt, *Religion, Politics, and Diversity* (Ithaca, N.Y., c. 1967), p. 175. The most recent and detailed treatment of this episode is Vincent P. Lannie, *Public Money and Parochial Education: Bishop Hughes, Governor Seward, and the New York School Controversy* (Cleveland, 1968).

14. Quoted in Leo Pfeffer, *Church, State, and Freedom* (Boston, 1953), pp. 295–296.

15. For a narrative of the early phase of the controversy, see "Religion in the Cincinnati Schools," *Old and New,* Vol. I (1870), pp. 122–124; this may well have been written by A. D. Mayo. The final decision of the Ohio Supreme Court is in the case of *Board of Education v. Minor et al.,* 23 Oh. St. 211, in Howe, pp. 322–329.

16. For a full account of the controversy, see Robert Michaelson, "Common School, Common Religion? A Case Study in Church-State Relations, Cincinnati, 1869–70," *Church History,* Vol. XXXVIII (1969), pp. 201–217. There is a sketch of Mayo in the *Dictionary of American Biography.* Vickers was born in England in 1835, came to this country in 1849, graduated from Meadville Theological School in 1863, studied at Heidelberg from 1863 to 1866, and became minister of the Cincinnati church in 1867. For details of his unhappy personal life, and turbulent later career as librarian of the Cincinnati Public Library and Rector of the University of Cincinnati, see Reginald C. McGrane, *The University of Cincinnati* (New York, c. 1963), Ch. 8.

17. Bellows to E. E. Hale, April 11, 1865. M.H.S.

18. A. D. Mayo, *Religion in the Common Schools: Three Lectures* (Cincinnati, 1869), p. 12.

19. A. D. Mayo, "What Does the Bible Represent in the American Common School?" *Universalist Quarterly,* Vol. XXI (1874), pp. 270, 273, 274.

20. *Proceedings of the Third Annual Meeting of the Free Religious Association* (Boston, 1870), pp. 52–53.

21. *Report of the Fifth Meeting of the National Conference . . . Oct. 22, 23, 24, and 25, 1872* (Salem, 1873), pp. 178–180.

22. "The National Church," *Old and New*, Vol. I (1870), p. 331. Since Edward Everett Hale was the editor of the magazine, and had to write much of it himself, the essay may have been by him. Interestingly enough, A. D. Mayo had written in somewhat the same vein in *Theology in America* (Albany, 1857); and someone (was it Bellows?) had referred to the Liberal Christian Church as "the American Church" which was the real rival of Catholicism in the competition to take over the position forfeited by Protestantism with its "un-American" theology. See *Address of the Council of the National Conference* (New York, 1868), p. 19.

23. So far as I have been able to discover, the generally conservative Christian theology of the Universalists made them sympathetic to Mayo's position. See, for example, A. J. Patterson, "Christian Calling," *Minutes of the Universalist General Convention* (New York, 1879), pp. 57–61.

24. *Christian Register*, Vol. LXXX (1901), p. 610.

25. J. H. Crooker, "Report of Committee on Non-sectarian Education," *Christian Register*, Vol. LXXXI (1902), p. 786.

26. Joseph Henry Crooker, *Religious Freedom in American Education* (Boston, 1903), pp. 26, 36, 37, 78.

INDEX

Abbot, Francis Ellingwood: 106–107,
119
Abbot, John Emery: 40
Absolute Religion: Parker's concept
of, 89, 90
Adams, John: 4
Adams, John Quincy: 67
Addison, Joseph: 1
Age of Reason: 1, 5
Alcott, A. Bronson: 66
Allen, Ethan: 3
Allen, Joseph: 46
Allen, Joseph Henry: 95, 108
Allyn, John: 132
American and Foreign Anti-Slavery So-
ciety: 64
American Anti-Slavery Society: 64, 66
American Colonization Society: 65, 67–
68, 76, 132
American Sunday School Union: 116
American Unitarian Association: inade-
quately supported, 86, 92–93; De-
cember 1864 meeting of, 92–94; re-
ports to New York convention, 102;
sponsors report on education, 122–
123; mentioned, 69
Ames, Charles G.: 104
Andrew, John A.: 99, 101, 102, 136
Antioch College: 71, 93, 94, 95
Arminianism: of Dudleian lecturers, 18;
at Harvard College, 26
Atonement, doctrine of: 12
Austin, Richard: 129
Autumnal Convention, Unitarian: 92,
99

Baptists: exempt from religious taxes,
111; attack Standing Order, 112–113
Barnard, John: 11, 14
Barnard, Thomas: 14–15
Barnes, David: 11, 13

Bartol, Cyrus A.: appraises character of
Bellows, 70, 85, 109; religious views
of, 87, 97; preaches for Emerson,
128
Bates, Joshua: 29
Bellows, Anna L.: 100
Bellows, Henry W.: antislavery views
of, 65, 72–75, 82, 131; and Sanitary Commission, 71, 81, 85, 95,
104; personality and leadership of,
70–72, 84–85, 92, 95; and Antioch
College, 71, 93, 94, 95; early career
of, 81–82; relations of, with Frothingham, 81, 97–98, 105, 137; appraises Unitarian denomination, 82–
92, 94, 96; and Christian Inquirer,
82, 95; letters of, to Hale, 83, 86,
88–89, 95, 98, 99–100, 103; letters
of, to members of family, 83, 86,
87, 94, 105; letter of, to Dewey, 84;
letters of, to Hedge, 87, 88; letters
of, to Clarke, 87, 90, 91; and creedal
issue, 88–91, 96, 101, 104, 107;
Christian loyalties of, 89–91, 100,
104; doctrine of Church of, 90–91;
relations of, with "radicals," 90, 104;
plans for New York convention, 93–
100; and Meadville Theological
School, 93, 94, 95; participates in
New York convention, 100–104;
achievement of, 108–109; mentioned, 119
Bellows, Mrs. Henry W.: 100
Bellows, Russell N.: 83
Belsham, Thomas: 26
Benevolence, disinterested: 28
Bentley, William: 4, 18
Bible reading: in Massachusetts schools,
116–117; in Cincinnati schools, 118–
120; rejected by Unitarians, 120–
121

Biblical criticism: studied at Harvard, 46
Boston (Massachusetts): Federal St. Church, 31
—First Church, 97
—Hollis St. Church, 92
—King's Chapel, 29
—Old South Church, 30
—Park St. Church, 31
—Second Church, 42, 45, 48
—South Congregational Society, 92
—West Church, 97
Brigham, Charles H.: 94–95
British moralists: 1
Broadway Atheneum: 101
Brooks, Caroline: 57
Buchanan, James: 68
Buckminster, Joseph Stevens: 29, 40
Burns, Anthony: 65, 78
Butler, Bishop Joseph: 17

California: Unitarian growth in, 83, 93, 94
Calvinism: moderate, 18, 25; moral argument against, 33
Campbéll, Alexander: 16
Campbell, George: 17
Carter, Artemas: 94
Catholics: oppose Protestant ethos in public schools, 117–118; opposed by Unitarians, 119–120, 121
Chadwick, John White: his biography of Channing, 23, 24, 30; at New York convention, 98, 101, 109; on Church and State, 120
Channing, Henry: 25–26
Channing, William Ellery: Dudleian Lecture of, 18, 39; Supernatural Rationalism of, 20, 39; intellectual background of, 23–28; preaches Codman ordination sermon, 28–29; and liberal Christians, 29–33; 127; attitude of, toward Calvinism, 32–33; Transcendentalist tendencies of, 34–38; sermon of, entitled "Likeness to God," 34, 38; antislavery stand of, 65, 72; defends Standing Order, 112, 113; on public education, 116; mentioned, 42, 76, 78
Channing, William Henry: 24, 32
Chauncy, Charles: 4

Christian Examiner: 95, 108, 113
Christian Inquirer: 69, 73, 82, 95, 99
Christian Register: 106
Church, doctrine of: 87, 89
Church and State: as related in Standing Order, 110–115; and public education, 115–122; Unitarian consensus on, 122–123
Church of All Souls (New York): 71, 72, 74, 81
Church of England: 18
Church of the Messiah (New York): 51, 65, 75, 99, 101
Church of the Redeemer (Cincinnati): 119
Cincinnati (Ohio): controversy over Bible reading, 118–120
—First Congregational Unitarian Church: 119
"Civic religion": 123
Civil War: effect of, on religious scene, 82, 92, 108
Clapp, Theodore: 64, 131
Clark, Peter: 9, 10–11
Clarke, James Freeman: antislavery views of, 64, 69, 132; condemns Unitarian individualism, 91; Convention sermon of, 98–99, 100, 106; seeks inclusiveness, 103; mentioned, 87, 107
Clarke, Samuel: 5, 17
Codman, John: 28–29
Collins, Anthony: 2
Colonization: 65, 132. *See also* American Colonization Society
Compromise of 1850: 75. *See also* Fugitive Slave Law, Seventh of March Address
Concord (Massachusetts): 43, 46, 60
—Unitarian Church and Parish: 41, 60
Congregationalism: 85–86, 87, 101
Constitution of Massachusetts: 111, 113
Constitution of the U.S.: as proslavery document, 68
Conway, Moncure D.: 119, 132
Cooke, George Willis: 62
Cooke, Samuel: 9–10
Crandall, Prudence: 66
Creedal issue: 87, 88–91, 96, 101, 103–104, 105–107

Crooker, Joseph Henry: 122–123

Davies, Samuel: 19
Dawes, Thomas: 31
Deism: 2–5
De Normandie, James: 119–121
Depravity of man: 30
Dewey, Orville: antislavery views of, 69, 75–76, 132; defended by Bellows, 70; and Fugitive Slave Law, 74, 77–78; doctrinal views of, 76; mentioned, 40, 51, 65
Dickinson, Jonathan: 19
Dirks, John Edward: 34
Disunion: 74–75
Divinity School Address: composition of, 54–56; reception of, 58; mentioned, 20, 36, 41
Dover (New Hampshire) Unitarian Church: 107
Dudleian lectureship: 7
Dudley, Chief Justice Paul: 5, 7
Dwight, John Sullivan: 45, 48
Dwight, Timothy: 2, 18

East Lexington (Massachusetts) Unitarian Church: 43, 45, 46, 48, 49
Edgell, David: 24, 34, 38
Edwardeanism: 23. *See also* Hopkinsianism, New Divinity
Edwards, Jonathan: 3, 26
Eliot, Christopher R.: 133
Eliot, Frederick May: 133
Eliot, Thomas D.: 107
Eliot, William G.: 102, 103, 107
Ellery, William: 29, 30
Ellis, George E.: 86, 105, 109
Ellis, Rufus: 86, 97, 105, 109
Emerson, Charles Chauncy: 43
Emerson, Edward Bliss: 36
Emerson, Lidian: 46, 48
Emerson, Mary Moody: 43
Emerson, Ralph Waldo: Transcendentalism of, 20, 36, 47; comments on Boston Unitarianism, 39; and Divinity School Address, 40, 54–56, 58; his relationships with Frost, 42, 55–56, 58–59, 60; preaches at East Lexington, 43, 45, 46, 49; criticizes bad preaching, 43–44, 46, 49–50, 53, 54, 59; and pastoral duties, 45, 48;

seeks eloquence, 45, 49; trained in Christian evidences, 47; as lecturer, 47–48, 49; vocational problem of, 48, 55; later churchgoing of, 59–60, 61; "Preaching Record" of, 128, 129; mentioned, 66, 83
Emerson, Waldo: 43, 46
Enlightenment. *See* Age of Reason
Enthusiasm: 12
Evangelical religion: 2–5
Evidences of Christianity: in thought of supernatural rationalists, 13–15; studied by Channing, 27; preached by Frost, 46–47; accepted by Emerson, 47; defended by Norton, 89

Fall of man: 10
Farmer, Hugh: 17
Federal St. Church (Boston): 31
Ferguson, Adam: 24, 26, 27, 28
Fillmore, Millard: 69
First Cause, argument from: 8
First Church in Boston: 97
First Congregational Unitarian Church (Cincinnati): 119
Fish, William H.: 132
Francis, Convers: 36–37, 132
Franklin, Benjamin: 3
Freeman, James: 4, 29
Free Religion. *See* "Radicals"
Free Religious Association: 99, 119, 120
Free Soil Convention: 68
Fremont, John C.: 68, 74
Friend of Progress: 105–106
Frost, Barzillai: early career of, 41–43; preaching of, 43, 44, 46, 49–50, 58, 59; pastoral qualities of, 45, 52; antislavery views of, 45, 132; doctrinal views of, 46–47; Emerson's attitude toward, 55–56, 58–59, 60; tutors James Russell Lowell, 56–58; illness and death of, 60–61
Frost, Mrs. Barzillai: 57, 130
Frothingham, Frederick: 132
Frothingham, Nathaniel Langdon: 36, 39
Frothingham, Octavius Brooks: his biography of his father, 39; his relationship with Bellows, 97–98, 137; criticizes New York convention, 105;

Frothingham, Octavius Brooks (*Cont.*) antislavery activity of, 132; mentioned, 81

Fugitive Slave Law: Dewey's views of, 70, 74, 75–78; mentioned, 65, 69

Fuller, Hiram: 45

Furness, William H.: 64, 105, 132

Gannett, Ezra Stiles: antislavery record of, 65, 69, 132; and New York convention, 86, 96–97, 98, 100, 109; on sectarianism, 139

Garrison, William Lloyd: 64, 66, 67, 68

Gay, Ebenezer: 4, 9, 10, 11

German Idealism: 20

Gilman, Samuel: 63, 71

Gloucester (Massachusetts) First Parish: 114

Gloucester (Massachusetts) Universalist Church: 113–114

God, proof of existence of: 8

Goddard, Harold C.: 35, 38

Great Awakening: 2, 17

Hackley School: 122

Hale, Edward Everett: writes to Bellows, 87, 96–97, 98; helps plan New York convention, 93–100; comments on Frothingham, 98; participates in convention, 100–104; mentioned, 87, 100, 103

Hale, Nathan: 57

Harris, Thaddeus Mason: 29

Harvard College: Dudleian Lectures at, 7; Channing a student at, 26

Harvard Divinity School: teachers and students of, 42, 43, 82, 132; and biblical criticism, 46; vitality of, 55; mentioned, 51, 72

Hawthorne, Nathaniel: 36, 60

Hedge, Frederic Henry: 52, 87, 108, 109, 129

Higginson, Thomas Wentworth: 64, 69, 74, 132

Hill, Alonzo: 86

Hoar, E. Rockwood: 57

Hoar, Samuel: 131

Holland, Frederick May: 133

Holland, Frederick W.: 132, 133

Hollis St. Church, Boston: 92

Holmes, John Haynes: 62

Holyoke, Edward: 7–9, 10

Hopkins, Samuel: 23–25, 26, 28

Hopkinsianism: 24, 25, 28. *See also* Edwardeanism, New Divinity

Hosmer, George W.: 94, 95

Hughes, Bishop John J.: 118

Hume, David: 15, 26, 27

Hutcheson, Francis: 24, 26, 28

Index, The: 119

Intuition: as source of religious truth, 20, 47

Jefferson, Thomas: 2, 3

Jesus Christ, historicity of: 13

Johnson, Samuel (of King's College): 4, 18

Johnson, Samuel (1822–1882): 138

Kendall, James: 132

Kidder, Henry P.: 92, 93, 94

King, T. Starr: 83, 93

King's Chapel (Boston): 29

Koch, G. Adolf: 4

Ladu, Arthur I.: 35, 37–38

Lardner, Nathaniel: 13, 17, 18

Leland, John: 26

Liberal Christianity: 91, 94

Liberal Christians: 28–30, 31. *See also* Arminianism

Liberal Church of America: 96, 102, 105, 106

Liberty Party: 68

Livermore, Abiel A.: 99

Locke, John: political theory of, 2; psychology of, 3, 8, 11–12, 20, 37; religious ideas of, 5; mentioned, 1, 17, 56, 58

Lothrop, Samuel K.: 84, 86

Lovejoy, Elijah: 68

Low, Abiel A.: 94, 101, 102, 104

Lowe, Charles: 92, 93

Lowell, Charles: 29, 52, 54, 56

Lowell, James Russell: 56–58

Majority: attitude of, toward minorities, 110, 113, 115

Mann, Horace: antislavery record of, 67, 69; on religion in schools, 116–117
Massachusetts Abolition Society: 64
Massachusetts Anti-Slavery Society: 64, 66, 69, 78–79
Massachusetts Board of Education: 116
Massachusetts Constitution: 111, 113
Massachusetts Historical Society: 81
Mather, Cotton: 4, 17
Mather, Increase: 17
May, Joseph: 133
May, Samuel Joseph: antislavery activities of, 64, 66–69, 132, 133; and Unitarians, 62, 69, 78–79
May, Samuel, Jr.: 64, 66, 133
Mayhew, Jonathan: 4, 18
Mayo, Amory D.: on Unitarian divisions, 109; on Church and State, 119–120
McGiffert, Arthur C.: 5
Meadville Theological School: 93, 94, 95
Methodism: 2
Mexican War: 65, 73
Miles, Henry A.: 44, 46–47
Miracles: as proof of revealed religion, 14–15, 18, 47, 52
Morality: rational proofs of, 9; as essential to good citizenship, 112–114, 123
Morse, Jedidiah: 31
Morse, Sidney H.: 119
Motte, Mellish I.: 131
Muelder, Walter G.: 3
Murray, John: 113–114

"National Church": 121–122, 123
National Conference of Unitarian Churches: plans for organization of, 93–100; organizing convention of, 100–104; name and Preamble of, 103, 105–107; considers Church-State issue, 119–122; mentioned, 81
Natural Religion: 3, 4, 7–11
New Divinity: 18. *See also* Edwardeanism, Hopkinsianism
Newell, William W.: 109
New England Anti-Slavery Society: 66
Newport, Rhode Island: 25, 27

Newton, Sir Isaac: 1, 3, 8, 20
New York convention: tests Unitarian vitality, 88; preparations for, 92–100; events of, 100–104; results of, 104–108
New York (N.Y.) Church of All Souls: 71, 72, 74, 81
—Church of the Messiah, 51, 65, 75, 99, 101
—Public School Society, 117–119
Nonviolence: 68
Norton, Andrews: 34, 40, 46, 89
Noyes, George R.: 46

Old and New: 119
Old South Church (Boston): 30
Olmstead, Clifton: 2
Osgood, Samuel: 69, 101, 107

Packard, Frederick A.: 116–117
Paine, Tom: 2, 3, 4
Paley, William: 17
Palmer, Elihu: 3
Park St. Church (Boston): 31
Parker, Nathan: 40, 132
Parker, Theodore: religious views of, 24, 34, 37, 89; antislavery views of, 64, 67, 132; causes Unitarian divisions, 83–84; mentioned, 68, 69
Parkman, Francis: 65, 132
Patterson, Robert Leet: 24
Patten, William: 25
Peabody, Andrew Preston: 109
Peabody, Oliver W. B.: 132
Pierce, John: 26, 31–32, 127
Pierpont, John: 132
Pillsbury, Parker: 67
Pochman, Henry A.: 35
Pope, Alexander: 2
Potter, William J.: 92
Pratt, Enoch: 94, 95
Prayer: in public schools, 110
Presbyterians: and Supernatural Rationalism, 18–19
Price, Richard: 26
Priestley, Joseph: 26, 27, 46
Princeton College: 19
Prophecy: fulfillment of, 14
Prospect Hill School: 122

Public School Society (New York): 117–118
Putnam, George: 79, 105

"Radicals": in Unitarian body, 83–84, 91, 105; oppose creedalism, 87–88; disagree with Bellows, 90
Randall, John H., Jr.: 6
Rationalism. *See* Deism, Supernatural Rationalism, Rational Supernaturalism
Rational Supernaturalism: 124–125. *See also* Supernatural Rationalism
Reason, Transcendental: 36, 47
Reid, Thomas: 26
Religion: social value of, 111–114, 121, 123
Revealed Religion: defended in Dudleian lectures, 11–15
Revelation: doctrine of, 12–13
Reynolds, Grindall: 61
Riley, I. Woodbridge: 4
Ripley, Ezra: 42, 43, 46, 53, 59, 132
Ripley, George: 35
Ripley, Samuel: 48
Robbins, Chandler: 97, 105, 109
Rosenmüller, E. F. K.: 46
Rousseau, Jean-Jacques: 2

San Francisco (California) Unitarian Church: 83
Sanitary Commission, U. S.: 71, 81, 82, 85, 95
Sargent, John T.: 132
Sawyer, Warren: 92
Schleusner, J. F.: 46
Schneider, Herbert W.: 23–24, 28, 34
Schools, public: and democratic citizenship, 115–116, 119–120, 123
Schultz, Arthur R.: 35
Scotch Realism: 20
Sears, Edmund Hamilton: 86, 109
Sears, Laurence: 3
Second Church in Boston: 42, 45, 48, 97
Secularism: 120–121
Seventh of March Address: 73
Sewall, Samuel E.: 66
Seward, William H.: 117
Shackford, Charles C.: 77
Sherman, John: 26

Silsbee, William: 48, 129
Simmons, George F.: 72, 131
Smith, Gerrit: 67, 68
Smith, H. Shelton: 35, 37
Social compact: 2
South Congregational Society (Boston): 92
Standing Order: Unitarian support of, 110–112, 114–115; minority attack on, 112–114; mentioned, 86
Staples, Carlton A.: 91
Stebbins, Rufus P.: 92–93, 95
Stephenson, George: 2
Sterne, Laurence: 2
Stetson, Caleb: 42
Stevens, Benjamin: 13
Stiles, Ezra: 19, 25
Stone Chapel (Boston): 29
Stuart, Moses: 31
Supernatural Rationalism: defined, 5–6, 15–16; in Dudleian lectures, 6–15; widespread acceptance of, 16–20; of Barzillai Frost, 46–47; of Emerson, 47. *See also* Rational Supernaturalism
Sweet, William Warren: 2
Syracuse convention: 103, 107

Taggart, Charles M.: 131
Tappan, David: 26
Taxes, parish: 111–114
Taylor, Isaac: 46
Texas, annexation of: 76
Thompson, James W.: 86
Thoreau, Henry David: 131
Thoreau, John: 131
Tillotson, Archbishop John: 5, 17
Towne, Edward C.: 81, 102, 107–108
Transcendental Club: 35, 42
Transcendentalism: distinguishing marks of, 34–36
Transcendentalists: 34–37, 89
Tuckerman, Joseph: 40

Understanding: as defined by Transcendentalists, 36, 47
Unitarianism: divisions within, 83–89, 105, 109; opportunity for expansion of, 82–84, 91–92, 94, 96; conservative wing of, 83–84, 87, 89, 91, 96–97, 101, 104; parochialism of, 85–

Unitarianism (*Cont.*)
86, 87. *See also* "Radicals," Transcendentalists
Unitarians: Supernatural Rationalism of, 16; antislavery record of, 62–63, 64–65; support Standing Order, 110–112, 114–115; approve Horace Mann's policies, 116
United States Sanitary Commission. *See* Sanitary Commission
Universalist Quarterly: 119
Universalists: attack Standing Order, 113–114; on Church and State, 140

Vickers, Thomas: 119–120, 123, 139

Walker, James P.: 93
Wasson, David A.: 132

Ware, Henry, Jr.: on Channing's Codman sermon, 32, 34; as successful pastor, 42, 52; mentioned, 40, 54
Ware, Henry, Sr.: 31, 32
Waterston, Robert C.: 77, 132
Watts, Isaac: 26
Webster, Daniel: 69, 73, 74, 76
Weiss, John: 105
Werkmeister William H.: 3
West Church (Boston): 97
Western Conference: 102
Whicher, Stephen: 58
Willard, Joseph: 26
Wilmot Proviso: 76
Wise, John: 17
Witherspoon, John: 3, 19–20

Yale College: 2